Healing Breath

For Florian and Benjamin

HEALING BREATH
Zen for Christians and Buddhists in a Wounded World

RUBEN L.F. HABITO

WISDOM PUBLICATIONS • BOSTON

Wisdom Publications
199 Elm Street
Somerville MA 02144 USA
www.wisdompubs.org

Library of Congress Cataloging-in-Publication Data

Habito, Ruben L. F., 1947–
  Healing breath : Zen for Christians and Buddhists in a wounded world / Ruben L.F. Habito. — [Rev. and updated ed.].
    p. cm.
  Previously published: Maria Kannon Zen Center Publications, 2001.
  Includes bibliographical references and index.
  ISBN 0-86171-508-X (pbk. : alk. paper)
  1. Spiritual life—Zen Buddhism. 2. Spiritual healing—Zen Buddhism. 3. Zen Buddhism—Doctrines. I. Title.
  BQ9288.H33 2006
  294.3'444—dc22

                    2006015194

ISBN 0–86171–508–X
First Printing
10 09 08 07 06
 5   4   3   2   1

Cover design by Jim Zaccaria, Interior design by Trice Atkinson. Set in AGarmond 12/15 pt.

Wisdom Publications' books are printed on acid-free paper and meet the guidelines for permanence and durability of the Production Guidelines for Book Longevity set by the Council on Library Resources.

Printed in the United States of America.

♻ This book was produced with environmental mindfulness. We have elected to print this title on 50% pcw recycled paper. As a result, we have saved the following resources: 20 trees, 14 million btus of energy, 1,728 lbs. of greenhouse gases, 7,171 gallons of water, and 921 lbs. of solid waste. For more information, please visit our web site, www.wisdompubs.org

CONTENTS

PREFACE

Zen is now a significant feature of the spiritual landscape in the West. In its original setting, Zen refers to a rigorous, demanding, and yet exhilarating form of spiritual discipline in the context of a Buddhist monastic way of life that flourished in East Asian societies.[1] In popular usage in the West, the term "Zen" has taken on an exotic air, and has come to be associated with certain styles or modes, as in "the Zen of cooking," "the Zen of golf," "the Zen of driving," and the like. The well-worn joke about the Zen hot dog—"one with everything"—is also indicative of the way it is perceived.

These popularized associations of "Zen," while sometimes on the outlandish side, are not entirely unrelated to the original setting out of which the term came about. This book, cognizant of its historical background in Buddhist monastic life in East Asian societies, presents Zen as a spiritual practice which opens one to a new way of seeing, and way of life in consonance with this way of seeing. It may hopefully inspire some readers to seek out a community of practice near their area. (Zen centers of various lineages can now be found in most major cities or in various places in North America and Europe, and in other parts of the world as well, and may be located through the yellow pages of a local phonebook or with a simple internet search.)

It is written especially for those who seek a spiritual path that leads to *healing* in the personal, social, and ecological dimensions of our being. If you are seeking guidelines for practice that connects these three dimensions of our being, this book is for you. If you seek wholeness, groundedness, and integrity in your life, to overcome a state of fragmentation or lack of direction in which you find yourself—*Healing Breath* is offered to you.

Perhaps you, too, have come to realize, with many others, that our world, our global community is in a sad state of affairs, going from bad to worse each day. In response to this state of affairs, you may already be engaged in some form of social, political, or ecological action, seeking to transform the way we live and relate to one another and to the Earth. You may also be one of those who feel overwhelmed by the magnitude of the task. If you've been tempted to pessimism or have thrown up your hands in despair when your best efforts don't seem to make a dent, this book has something for you.

The spiritual path that leads to healing begins with a change in our *way of seeing*. According to Father Thomas Berry—a twentieth century prophet, and witness to our Earth's woundedness and the urgent need to take it seriously—our basic problem is not one of strategy, but *cosmology*.[2] The following chapters trace our global malaise to a misguided cosmology. Our mistaken view of ourselves and our world begets destructive attitudes and violent behavior toward one another and toward the Earth itself.

Seeing that our ailing socio-ecological condition is fundamentally rooted in an *erroneous view* of things, we can also see that healing begins with a *right* view.[3] This book describes a step-by-step healing process that can begin right here and now. Using the concrete situations of our everyday life, we can move toward a right view and toward a right way of living together on this planet.

Unfortunately, the spiritual path and the path of socio-ecological transformation are often regarded as unrelated human endeavors. Many who have avidly pursued one have no particular interest in the other. Growing numbers of us realize, however, that these two human dimensions are vitally connected. *Healing Breath* offers a way to integrate a spiritual path with active, socio-ecological engagement as the ground.

Healing the woundedness of Earth is not unrelated to healing our personal woundedness. The wounds of Earth and those of the individuals making up our Earth community cannot be separated. Thus healing in our individual lives becomes the basis for the healing of the whole Earth.

This book also addresses another set of questions. In Zen retreats over the years I have been asked: What kind of belief system is required to fully engage in Zen practice? Can a Christian practice genuine Zen? In other words, is Zen practice compatible with a Christian faith commitment? If so, how can such a spiritual practice in an Eastern tradition inform Christian life and understanding? Challenged and prodded on by such questions, I was inspired to write this book as a way of responding to them.[4]

I also want to address questions posed to me by Buddhist friends and colleagues. Some of them, born and raised in Jewish or Christian traditions, have written off their Judaism or Christianity as no longer pertinent to their outlook and way of life. Indeed, many Buddhists regard any form of theistic religious expression as an unhelpful worldview, an erroneous belief system, or unfruitful practice. Their question to me is "How can you practice Zen as you do and still remain a Christian?"

In the process of describing what is involved in the Zen way of life, I will consider various Christian expressions, symbols, and practices—not as an apologetic for a belief system, but as a way of suggesting how these expressions, etc., from Jewish and Christian traditions, too, point to transformative and healing perspectives and experiences opened to one in Zen practice.

In the 1970s, as I sat in *zazen* at the San-Un Zendo in Kamakura, Japan, I was receiving the regular guidance of Zen Master Koun Yamada. As he led me by the hand through the intricacies of the Zen path through koan practice, he asked me to share with him any insights or perspectives I found in the Bible or on the Christian spiritual path, especially in the Spiritual Exercises of St. Ignatius that I was familiar with from my Jesuit training, that related to what I was learning in my Zen practice. Writing this book has given me the opportunity to recover and reflect once more on some of those insights and perspectives, and to share them with Buddhist, Jewish, and Christian friends and readers.

This book is a personal testimony of an experience of "*intra-religious dialogue*": the encounter of two (or more) religious traditions within the same individual.[5] In this kind encounter, we are invited to place ourselves *within* differing religious traditions, to possibly discover mutual resonance as they illuminate or mutually challenge one another.

More and more of us are engaging in this adventure. And as we do so, we are able to open our eyes to the treasures within the religious traditions that coexist in our global village, and find great fruit in the endeavor. We are coming to realize that we have many allies in our common concern for healing ourselves and healing the Earth, whom we can recognize across religious boundaries.[6]

A polarized global society wracked in pain calls out for the caring engagement of all it members, no matter what religious tradition, if any, we belong to. This book reflects on the healing power of Zen, a gift to the world from the Buddhist tradition. Zen is a form of spiritual practice, a way of life, and a vision of reality that not only can launch us in our inner work of personal healing, but also at the same time enhance and intensify our engagement in tasks of global healing.

ACKNOWLEDGMENTS

I would like to thank Josh Bartok and the staff of Wisdom Publications, as well as Helen Berliner, for their efforts on this new volume, *Healing Breath*—a thoroughly revised and updated edition of a book previously published by Orbis Books in 1993, and by Maria Kannon Zen Center Publications in 2001, under the title *Healing Breath: Zen Spirituality for a Wounded Earth*. I also thank Bill Burrows and Robert Ellsberg of Orbis, who allowed the publication of the previous Orbis edition, and Helen Cortes, who supervised the publication of the Maria Kannon Zen Center edition.

The earlier publication came out of reflections based the experience of participating in, assisting at, and also directing Zen retreats over many years, since my first sesshin at Engaku-ji Temple in Kita-Kamakura, Japan, in May of 1971. Soon after that first taste of Zen, at the urging of my Jesuit spiritual director, the late Fr. Thomas Hand, S.J., I joined the Zen community practicing in San-Un Zendo (Zen Hall of the Three Clouds) in Kamakura, and was accepted by Koun Yamada Roshi as a student. To my Teacher, Koun Yamada, as well as to his successors, Jiun Kubota and Ryoun Yamada, I express profound thanks. To all my

Jesuit mentors, including Fr. Hand, and also Fr. Hugo Enomiya-Lassalle, Fr. Kakichi Kadowaki, Fr. Heinrich Dumoulin, and many others who have inspired me and guided me in their own ways in the spiritual path, I offer this book with heartfelt gratitude.

To the late Fr. Benigno Mayo, S.J., who admitted me into the Society of Jesus in the Philippines, and to the late Fr. Pedro Arrupe, S.J., who as General of the Society, assigned me to Japan in 1970, my undying gratefulness. Here I also express my ongoing gratitude and warm fraternal sentiments to the members of the Jesuit Provinces in the Philippines and in Japan, who took me in as one of their own for twenty-five precious years of my life.

To the countless friends and benefactors and companions along the way, I wish to convey my deep appreciation and gratitude for the multitudes of ways they have supported me and kept me going in this path. Just to list down their names would take a whole book in itself, so I will desist from this here and will continue to cherish each of them in my heart. These include those whom I met in various visits to rural and urban communities in my own country, the Philippines, and in India, Indonesia, Thailand, Hong Kong, Taiwan, and Japan. It was in these visits that I was privileged to meet many persons in grassroots communities, those who bear the brunt of the unjust and destructive structures of the world, whose children continue to suffer from hunger and malnutrition, whose daughters are sent off to the big cities to seek their fortunes in ways we would prefer not to imagine. It was in those precious times spent with grassroots communities in different places that I have come face-to-face with the wounds we all bear as members of this Earth community. During those visits, and in their aftermath, I have been blessed to experience the power of cosmic compassion at work in various ways toward the healing of our wounded Earth.

The continuing friendship and support of Sr. Elaine MacInnes, OLM, Roshi and founder of Zen communities in Manila, Philippines, Oxford, England, and Toronto, Canada; of

Sr. Rosario Battung, RGS, a Dharma sister in the Sanbo Kyodan, and of Sr. Vicky Palanca, ICM, have been a source of strength and inspiration through the years.

Heartfelt gratitude also to Sr. Pascaline Coff, OSB, of the Osage Forest of Peace Monastery in Sand Springs, Oklahoma, who continues to invite me to direct annual retreats at their ashram, as well as to Sr. Priscilla, Sr. Benita, and all the sisters of her community, and to all of those who participated in those retreats through the years. I thank Fr. Richard Rohr, OFM, of the Center for Action and Contemplation in Albuquerque, New Mexico, and Christina Spahn, co-director, as well as Kathleen O'Malley, and the succeeding directors and staff of the Center, for the opportunity to assist at Encounter of the Heart retreats there over a number of years. The talks given at those retreats provided the kernel of the material that came to be developed in this book. I also thank the late Sr. Thelma Hall, RC, with fond memory, and Wendy Foulke, who provided opportunities to sit with their practice communities in the New York area, and Hugh and Susan Curran, who invited me to sit with their Zen group in Morgan Bay, Maine, several times.

All my Dharma sisters and brothers in our international Sanbo Kyodan Zen community have been and continue to be sources of inspiration and collegial support, and to each of them I offer my deep thanks, as I look forward to our annual gatherings.

The members of our Maria Kannon Zen Community have been my own companions on the path since I arrived in Dallas in 1989, and they have been my teachers in so many different ways. To all of them, especially those who gave of their own time and energy to serve on the Board of Directors through the years, including Lee Ann Nail, Roy Hamric, John Douglas, Dawne Schomer, Bob Curry, Don Champlin, Chris Runk, Helen Cortes, Susan Long, Joe Benenate, Mary Alice Binion, who each served terms as president. Deepest gratitude goes especially to Helen Cortes, our Executive Director, for her resilience and resourcefulness and tireless and caring service to the community, without whom we would not be where we are today.

I deeply thank my colleagues at Perkins School of Theology, Southern Methodist University, beginning with Dean James E. Kirby, who welcomed me into the faculty in the Fall of 1989; then Associate Dean James Ward and his spouse Miriam, and Sue Ferrell and Mary Ann Marshall, administrative staff, who all in their own caring ways made the move across the Pacific less traumatic than it could have been; H. Neill McFarland, my predecessor in this post; the late Frederick J. Streng, a pioneer in Buddhist Christian dialogue; William ("Billy") Abraham, always a challenging and stimulating partner in theological conversation, and his entire family; Charles Curran, for the warm friendship and inspiring example of an engaged academic thoroughly committed to his church and to the academy; Deans Robin Lovin and William B. Lawrence, and all the colleagues in the faculty and administrative staff, and all the students I have been blessed to encounter in and out of classroom contexts here at Perkins through the years. In particular, I thank Lucy Cobbe, who as gone out of her way on several occasions to help me with technical matters regarding this manuscript; and Stephanie Carroll, my assistant at the Associate Dean's office, who makes my own day-to-day work much more manageable through her able support.

As always, my untold gratitude to my father, Dr. Celestino P. Habito, Sr., and my mother, the late Faustina F. Habito; to my brothers Cielito and R. Celestino, Jr., and sisters Teresa Stuart and Maricel Cadiz and their families; to Maria Dorothea, beloved wife, friend, constructive critic, and Zen companion. I renew my prayer and hope that our two sons, Florian and Benjamin, may never falter in being grateful for this gift of life and for the gifts of Earth. May their hearts be open to hear the cries of the world, and may they be inspired and empowered to offer their lives as a response to what they hear.

Diagnosing Our Woundedness

RECOGNIZING OUR ailment is the first step toward healing. Healing cannot happen if we refuse to acknowledge the problem.[1] Taking a good look at the world around us and seeing the state it's in makes it difficult to maintain an attitude of denial.

Surveying Our Situation

The entire global community felt the impact of the attack on the World Trade Center towers in New York on September 11, 2001. This shocking event radically affected our view of the world, especially for North Americans. But from wider geographical and historical angles, we cannot but acknowledge that violent acts resulting in the loss of innocent lives, on varying scales of magnitude, have always been part of human history. At this very moment, armed conflicts are claiming human lives—for ethnic, compete with). Or they may be the media images bombarded into our subconscious, the "rich and famous" people we should emulate to become "a person of worth."

Our personal woundedness is brought home as we notice ourselves going through life in ways that aren't really true to who we are at bottom. We feel lack of acceptance for *who* we are, and are unable to feel at home *wherever* we are.

This lack of peace within may drive us to alcohol, drugs, wanton sexual activity, or some other form of diversion. But going in this direction only aggravates our brokenness. We may seek solace in unhealthy, co-dependent relationships, or turn to other time-killers like television, shopping, or even work. Various forms of addiction plague many of us, as we seek to hold on to something to cushion us from insecurity and from our inability to live authentic lives.

Our own brokenness, then, leads us to behave in ways that are destructive—for us, for others, and for life and the world in general. We inflict wounds upon one another as a way of retaliating for the personal wounds that have been inflicted upon us. It has been found that many convicted child molesters and other sexual abusers are themselves victims of abuse. Unhealed wounds within drive us to victimize those around us, beginning with those we love the most.

Taking a panoramic point of view, we can see the interconnectedness of our personal, social, and ecological wounds. This is what we mean by *wounded Earth:* Earth refers not only to the physical environment "out there," over which we presume to have some control or even mandate to "manage," or steward. Rather, Earth is the matrix of interconnected life itself: the mountains, rivers, and *all* sentient beings—including us humans who find ourselves at the heart of this web of life, as its consciousness.[4]

Earth is us and we are Earth. To speak of a "broken Earth" is to speak of our own brokenness; it is to speak of the woundedness of the very fabric of interconnected life. From this point of view, holes in the ozone layer are not just perforations in the sky; global warming is not just a thermal inconvenience. These are very real poisons and dangers threatening the flow of life itself. In the same way, the ethnic and ideological violence in our interconnected community affects us all—as does the woundedness that each of us feels deep within our soul.

Using psychological terms, this dysfunctional situation is in need of healing on many levels. In seeking to heal Earth's wounds, we are healing ourselves.[5]

Tracing the Roots of Our Brokenness

What is behind all this global, ecological, social, and personal woundedness? We need to look deeper to trace its root causes, and to see more clearly the steps we must take to heal it.

Other People

Jean-Paul Sartre wrote in his play *No Exit* that "Hell is other people." This succinct statement strikes a deep chord. It touches on one way we human beings regard one another.

I see others as impinging upon *my* freedom, as they subject me to their judgmental gaze or stand in the way of my desires. I find myself in a constant state of conflict with this "other," beginning with my parents, siblings, and the individuals I encounter on my journey through life.[6] This stance then extends to the groups I identify with: my neighborhood gang, ethnic group, economic class, or religious, national, or corporate community.

It is this stance that lies at the root of all violent conflict. "I" and "other" are at cross-purposes—over territorial rights, economic advantages, ideological differences, religious beliefs, or simple differences in lifestyle. Our differences may be as trivial as the way we break an egg (to cite a caricature from *Gulliver's Travels*). Conflicts are triggered by anything that demarcates "us" from "them."

At rock bottom, this "I" and "other" attitude is at the root of all the woundedness we create. Viewing our fellow human beings as "other," we exclude them from our field of concern. This allows us to go on living our cozy lives, preoccupied with our own affairs, indifferent to all else. What happens to the others "out there" doesn't concern us. Now and then, with a twinge of conscience, we may send a check to some organization to help the poor and less privileged. We breathe a sigh of thanks that it is us, not *our* children. We are blessed, unlike "those unfortunate others"—whom we may even include in our intercessory prayers.

The Natural World as Other

We have even come to view the natural world—the very source of our life and nurture—as "other." This destructive attitude has resulted in destructive acts toward the nature, which we view as an inimical wilderness to be tamed, controlled, and brought into submission for our human purposes.

So-called progress in science and technology has made the natural world an object of inquiry. Our measuring instruments have discovered much about its secrets and patterns of behavior. Sophisticated telescopes reach far into the galaxies; spaceships [probe] the outer areas of this solar system. We have split what was once considered to be an indivisible atom and continue to probe subatomic particles with our electron microscopes. Reaching down to the genetic level, we have even altered the makeup of human beings yet to be born. And all this has given us the impression that we are now in control.

Gifted with rationality, we human beings see ourselves at the pinnacle of a hierarchy of being. Our very use of language reveals our attitude towards nature as Other. We speak of our *environment,* or "that which is around us"—and that which surrounds us is subservient to our designs. As the disastrous effects of this view impinge on the natural world, the well-intentioned among us say that we must "protect" our environment; we must conserve our depleted resources.

Such voices may do us all a great service by calling our attention to the urgency our situation; they may even lead to beneficial action. But they are still based on the presupposition that is the root of our malady: nature is Other. And it's still "us" versus "them." They may emphasize the need to treat this Other kindly—for our own good. Then this Other will be kind to us. But the view of nature as Other does not address the root cause of our malady.[7] To paraphrase Thomas Berry, improvements in *strategy* will not make up for a fundamental gap in our *cosmology.*

Alienated Within My Own Self

The conventional attitude of "I" and "other" determines the way we project ourselves in the world. Upon the implicit premise that "I am here" and the rest of the world is "out there"—against me— we base our daily lives.

The existence of this "I" needs to be affirmed through the recognition of those around it, beginning with its first human contacts, its biological parents. And as embodied beings, we need food, clothing, and shelter to ensure our continued existence. Then we become conscious of needing and wanting more: more material goods, more affection, and more praise, esteem, and approbation. If these don't come easily, we devise ways to get noticed and obtain them—beginning within a few months of birth. As we grow wiser in the ways of the world, we employ more diverse and nuanced means to these ends. All the while, this I "in here" is separate from and set against the rest of the world "out there."

A few blessed ones among us have always been able to see through this veil of separation. The mystics, saints, and poets among us are able to experience a deeper dimension of reality. They can bridge the seeming opposition between the "I" and "other" of ordinary consciousness. They can see in an intimate way the interconnectedness between this subjective consciousness, or "I," and everything else.

Such individuals, living in many different times and places, bear witness to the inexhaustible possibilities and unfathomable grandeur of being human. These are persons who, in just being who they are, point all of us toward this dimension within us, wherein lies the source of our healing. By taking us beyond our ordinary way of looking at the world, they cut through our assumptions about the separation of "I" and "Other."[8]

Until we find our home in the "place" that overcomes this gap, each of us is consigned to a state of alienation. By identifying with a false and idealized image of self, we view the world as "other" and keep it at arms length. This alienated "I" is quite vulnerable and easily wounded when it doesn't get what it wants or needs—or when it gets what it doesn't want. To protect itself, it then creates a mask, or *persona,* to carry it through its dealings with others.

In moments of clarity, we can perhaps see how this idealized self image takes over us. This is the "I" that strives to meet the expectations of parents and peers; that is driven to keep up with the Joneses; that wants attention, and wants to control. But as long as we wear this mask, we only aggravate our woundedness. How does this separative I-consciousness (which we can also call "the egoic self," following Eckhart Tolle) actually cause our alienation?

First, our mode of being—as being-in-time—makes us constantly look toward the future for the fulfillment. In everything we do, we project into the realm of the not-yet, anticipating how our actions or external conditions might be made more favorable. But banking on the fulfillment of our desires makes us anxious about the future; and anxiety drives us to frantic efforts to better our conditions. Thus we bury ourselves in work, or in any of our myriad other ways of trying to cope with anxiety. We might look in nostalgic remembrance to the "good old days" and compare them with our present miserable state of affairs. Or we may look with resentment and regret at the past troubles that inexorably led to our present woes. Whether in anxious anticipation of the not-yet, or regret of the no-longer-there, or rueful recollection of the once-was—as beings "trapped" in linear time, we live in alienation from ourselves.

Second, as a subject viewing the physical world "out there," my own body becomes an objective reality outside of or seen in opposition to me. At odds with its own body, the separative I-consciousness regards it either with contempt (as in many ascetic traditions, as an obstacle to its ideal of "angelic purity"), or in contrast, as that which drives me to the pursuit of all kinds of pleasures and sensual desires. The body is taken as either something to be mastered and controlled, or to be allowed as much pleasure and sensual satisfaction as it is capable of. In either case, "I" and "my body" are seen as distinct and separate.

Third, we discriminate between what we perceive as desirable and undesirable, good and bad, beautiful and ugly, pleasurable and painful. As such, we are biased in favor of the desirable, good, beautiful, and pleasurable—and we reject their opposites. However, as psychologist C.G. Jung points out, the "other side" of these opposites, which he calls features of our *shadow*, are within all of us. When we suppress or repress our shadow side, we tend to project them onto others, with whom we then see ourselves in conflict. Thus, through rejection of aspects of our own being, we intensify hatred and opposition to "other" onto whom we have projected them.

Living under the sway of the separative I-consciousness compounds our experience of alienation from our home in our true, integrated self.

Overcoming the Separative I-Consciousness

Martin Heidegger pinpointed the basic malaise of Western society as a "forgetfulness of Being."[9] When human consciousness, or ego-as-subject, degenerates to the point of relating to beings *(Seiendes)* as objects, we confront a mode that has lost all connectedness with Being *(Sein)* itself. To reconnect with our living ground of Being, we must come to a mode of awareness that cuts through the subject-object dichotomy.

In Martin Buber's terms, this distorted way of being-in-the-world is the result of our "I-it" mode of awareness. Briefly, I-it refers to an "I," or subject, that views everything else in the world as "it," or object. By contrast, I-Thou awareness is a way of being that perceives the universe and all of its elements—human beings, trees, rocks—as "Thou." Unlike the I-it mode, the ground of I-Thou is a lived awareness of our connectedness with the universe. Encountering Thou, from the depth of my being, is a moment of revelation wherein this "I" is transformed.[10]

A diagnostic view of the human problematic and its resolution thus indicates that the separative I-consciousness, or egoic self, is at the root of all the different levels of our woundedness. Realizing this is also the key to our healing. But if this delusive egoic self that dominates all my attitudes and actions is not my true Self, what is? Who am I, if not this "I" that I am (self-)conscious of, standing in opposition to a world and its inhabitants "out there"? Finding out the answer to this question is perhaps the single most important task of our life.

The Role of Religions

Throughout the course of human history, we have sought answers to these fundamental questions: Who am I? Where do I come from? Where am I heading? What is the meaning of my life and all human life? What is the Good to be pursued above all? What is the nature of ultimate reality? What is my ultimate destiny, and what must I do in order to arrive at it? Immanuel Kant summed these issues up in three questions: What can I know? What ought I to do? What can I hope for? Countless thinkers throughout history have proposed various answers to these questions.

In the time of the Buddha, in the fifth century before the Common Era, there was a melee of philosophical opinions on the nature of things, on the way humans should comport themselves, and on what we could expect in terms of ultimate destiny—and the discussion has not abated.

The world's religions proffer answers to these central questions. It is the function of religion to give us a sense of meaning, belonging, identity, and some sense of cosmic affirmation. This is what enables us to go on living this fragile and mortal life—otherwise fraught with uncertainties—within an orderly, intelligible, and manageable framework. Sociologist Peter Berger refers to this role of religion as "the Sacred Canopy," an apt term for an enclosure that shields human beings from the onslaughts of the unbearable chaos and mystery of their existence.[11]

In times of turmoil, conflict, or external threat, a shared religious vision can unite people in community. Religious worldviews and the experiences associated with them can sustain our highest aspirations. And throughout the ages, religion has inspired the artistic spirit and drawn forth the creative energies of human beings. A broad survey of the world's cultural heritage would attest to the dominant role that religion plays in the flowering of human societies.

This same source of creative, cohesive energy, however, can become a source of conflict and violence. We need not go into the details here of the violence and cruelty perpetrated by human beings in the name of religion, documented by many recent works.[12]

People who seek clear-cut, definitive answers to their deep-seated questions can find a sense of purpose in affiliating with a religious community that offers well-defined and clear-cut answers to basic questions. However, it is all too easy to take these as answers "from above" in an unreflective, uncritical way. We then unwittingly appropriate a kind of triumphalistic self-confidence and authoritativeness that becomes divisive of the human community—"If you are not with us, you are against us."

Religion thus becomes a cause of conflict on the individual and communal levels. In this way, adherence to a religious tradition can aggravate, rather than alleviate, the woundedness of our human family. It can intensify and absolutize the rift between "us" (those who believe and belong) and "them" (those who don't). All too easily we can then slip into an attitude that dehumanizes or demonizes "them."

Historically, all acts violence and atrocities against many innocent people were only made possible by relegating these people, in the minds of the perpetrators, to the level of "unworthy objects," or to a status below human. In so many recorded cases, religious belief has supported such relegation of "others" to a status that could provide justification for their inhumane treatment, or their extermination—whether as "heretics," "witches," various animals or demons, or as simple nonentities.

In previous epochs, adherents of the same religious tradition could maintain their communal lives and uphold their shared views and values within distinct and demarcated geographical regions. In our twenty-first-century globalized society, adherents of different traditions now live in contiguity with one another, and interact with one another on different levels.[13] This fact itself calls for a renewed examination of the role of religion in our human community—if we're to have a shared future as a global family, and not bequeath a fractured, warring, desolate "Mad Max" type of world to our descendants.

The task of reexamining the role of the religions—with their tendencies toward divisiveness and conflict, but also with their empowering visions and their potential as forces for healing, wholeness, and cohesion—falls upon all of those who have found something to cherish and uphold in their respective religious traditions. Can the world's religious traditions make positive contributions toward the building of a truly global human family, rather than become factors that tend to pit human beings against one another, exacerbating further division, violence, and conflict, with their differing belief systems and values and practices? Such is a task being taken on by thinkers and spiritual leaders of different religious groups committed to their own religious perspective, in dialogue with members of other traditions. This book offers a small contribution in this direction, gleaning from elements found in two major religions, Buddhism and Christianity.

With acute awareness of the present woundedness of our human condition, we can now examine two prescriptions for healing, based on different yet complementary views of this woundedness. The first comes from the Buddhist tradition, the second from the Christian message as presented in Scriptures.

Four Ennobling Truths: A Buddhist Diagnosis

An ancient Indian medical tradition (the Ayurveda) works on a fourfold set of steps to heal the sick.

The first step involves a detailed diagnosis of the patient, examining the manifestations of the sickness, and its extent. If the patient has a skin eruption, for example, one doesn't just apply some balm and stop at that. Are other symptoms present? Do other parts hurt? Are other bodily functions not in order? A good physician doesn't jump immediately to just eradicating the symptoms by applying palliatives or temporary painkillers.

The second step is an investigation of the causes behind those symptoms. Is the eruption caused by an externally inflicted wound or by something else? The patient's diet, sleep, and exercise habits are possible factors. As the causes of the symptoms are pinpointed, the physician goes to the third step.

The third step is the envisioning of a healthy state of being. In this state, the skin eruption and pain have subsided. And the patient can go on living a normal life, in a way that will not lead to further eruptions or other complications.

The fourth step calls for taking practical measures toward such a healthy state of being. These might include external treatment to prevent further infection and pain, as well as regulation of the patient's diet, sleep, and so on.

In this way, not only are the symptoms of an ailment alleviated, but also the causes of those symptoms. Thus their recurrence is prevented and the patient can live a normal and healthy life.

These four steps from an ancient Indian medical tradition served as a framework for formulating a key Buddhist doctrine, the Four Ennobling Truths. Expounded by the Buddha shortly after attaining enlightenment, these four truths provide us with an understanding of the nature of enlightenment—not as concept, but as a praxis leading to a state of well-being and whole-being. (In Chapter 2 we will look at this practice more closely.)

The first Ennobling Truth is usually (and poorly) translated as "Life is suffering." This is the Buddha's diagnosis of the human situation. *Suffering* is the key word here, but it is much more nuanced than the English word *suffering*. The Sankrit word is *duhkha*. Etymologically, *kha* means the hub of a wheel; and the prefix *duh* is something like the English prefix "mis," as when we say something is "mis-placed" or "mis-taken." The word *duhkha,* therefore, points to a situation wherein the hub of a wheel is not properly centered; it is dislocated, and so the wheel is not functioning the way it should. The first Ennobling Truth is a basic recognition that all is not well with the way we are living our human lives. Another ingenious translation of *duhkha* is *dis-ease—* with the emphasis on the hyphen.

The second Ennobling Truth is that there is a cause for *duhkha.* This proposition leads to an inquiry into the root cause of the ailing human condition—a cause the Buddha identifies as craving.

Craving, in turn, is rooted in ignorance. This is a state of delusion about our existence, delusion based on the (false) assumption of a separate self. Ignorance is the belief in the *I, me, mine* standing vis-à-vis the world out there—and not cognizant of our fundamental interconnectedness with everything else.

The third Ennobling Truth affirms that *there is a way to extinguish duhkha.* This is an affirmation of the possibility of a wholesome state of being. The Sanskrit word is *nirodha,* synonymous with *nirvana,* which refers to the extinguishing of a flame. This is the key word expressing the third Ennobling Truth. It is helpful to set aside the popularized, stereotypical associations with the word *nirvana,* taken as "a state of total, final extinction," and rather, simply note that the term refers to the extinguishing of the basic cause, and thereby the manifestations of the dis-ease in our human condition.

The fourth Ennobling Truth points the way toward the state of well-being envisioned in the third Truth. It's presented as an eightfold Path, consisting of right seeing, right thought, right speech, right action, right livelihood, right effort, right mindfulness, and right concentration. Following the eightfold path opens to a life free from craving, whereby the fundamental ignorance about the nature of one's existence is dispelled at its root.

The eightfold Path is the Buddhist prescription for healing the ailing human condition. It recognizes the basic dis-ease of human existence, as expressed in the first Ennobling Truth. And it is geared toward recovering a state of well-being, with eight practical steps that serve as a systematic and concerted attack on the root cause of our ailment.[14]

The last three steps of the eightfold Path, namely right effort, right mindfulness, and right concentration, are key components of the Zen way of life. The first five steps can be seen as preparatory stages to cultivate the last three. Coming out of the Buddhist tradition, Zen derives its basic inspiration from the four Ennobling Truths and the Eightfold Path.

Sin and Salvation: The Christian Message

Where the Buddhist tradition expresses the human problem in terms of *duhkha,* or dissatisfaction and dis-ease, the Christian view sees the human condition as a state of sin.

Sin is a state of separation, or alienation, from God. In the Creation story of Genesis, man and woman were originally created in God's image. But, choosing their own selfish ways and separating themselves from God's plans, they place themselves in opposition to God. This separation from God—and the rest of creation—alienates man and woman from their true selves, as beings created in God's image.

An important point must be noted here: the *basic* premise of the Christian message is not that man and woman sinned, but that they were *originally created in God's image.* They were originally created in a state of grace, receiving divine blessing and enjoying divine presence in their lives. In the Genesis story, the

Fall came as man and woman, against divine will, ate of the "fruit of the tree of knowledge of good and evil." Thus they lost their state of grace through their own choice.

The term *original sin* is thus a gross misnomer and a misrepresentation of the more significant aspect of Christian teaching. It causes much misunderstanding and distorted attitudes outside and within Christian tradition, in giving the impression of a pessimistic view of human nature. We need to reclaim the vision of the Genesis story: our original condition is a state of grace. Being the image of God is what's "original" in our created being—not sin.[15]

Now, however—historically and existentially—we find ourselves in a state of sin, a state of separation from God. We are alienated from the very source of our life and its original blessing. This alienation from God can be called our "cosmic woundedness."

Separation from God can be seen on three levels. First, separation from God is manifested as alienation from our fellow human beings, who like ourselves are created in the image of God. Seeing others as objects, as opponents, as competitors, or means to our own selfish ends—this kind of alienation is at the root of the violence we perpetrate upon each other.

Second, we are in a state of alienation from the natural world, which is God's creation. Having separated ourselves from nature, we regard it as Other to us and in need of being subdued and dominated. Alienation from nature is the root of the ongoing global ecological crisis we all face.

Third, we are alienated from our own selves. Made in the image of God, we are unable to reflect that image in our awareness and in the way we live our lives, preoccupied as we are with our selfish goals based on our idealized and false self-images.

These various levels of alienation correspond with the state of existential woundedness described earlier. This is what we mean when we say that the human condition is in a state of sin and in need of salvation.

The word *salvation*—a key to understanding the Christian worldview—derives from the Latin word *salus,* or healthy and sound, which in turn derives from the Greek *holos,* meaning whole. The Christian Gospel, or Good News, is a message of salvation. Addressing us in our cosmic woundedness, it proclaims the Way to healing and wholeness.

By undergoing a total change of heart and mind, a *metanoia* (literally, "beyond consciousness"), we experience a renovation of our being as we are reconciled with God, with our true selves, with our fellow humans, and with the whole of creation.

Recalling the Buddhist expression of the human predicament in terms of *duhkha*—a state of dis-location, dis-ease, and of being out of touch with being itself—we can perceive a basic resonance with the Christian understanding of cosmic woundedness due to sin. How, then, in concrete terms, do we overcome *duhkha?* What constitutes the path of salvation from this state of sin? To address these questions, let us now look at some key features of Zen practice.

2

Tasting and Seeing—
The Zen Way of Life

W E BEGIN our description of Zen with a look at its four characteristic marks and the threefold fruit it bears forth into the life of a practitioner. We will then see that Zen is not an individualistic, navel-gazing kind of spirituality as it is sometimes stereotyped to be. Rather, Zen is a way of life and practice that opens to a new way of seeing who we are, and of our connection with all of reality. This new way of seeing is the key to healing our personal, social, and ecological woundedness.

Four Marks of Zen

Zen (*Ch'an* in Chinese) is distinguished by four marks or characteristics. This formulation of the four marks is attributed to Bodhidharma, the semi-legendary, sixth-century Buddhist monk from South India who is credited with introducing this form of practice and way of life into China.[1] The four marks of Zen are enshrined in the following verse:

A special transmission outside Scriptures
Not relying on words or letters
    Pointing directly to the human mind,
Sees into one's own true nature,
    thus becoming an Enlightened One.

Special Transmission Outside Scriptures

Zen attributes its origins to the enlightenment experience of Gautama Shakyamuni, the Buddha (from the Sanskrit verb *budh,* to awaken). The enlightenment experience of the Awakened One was preceded by six years of arduous searching and practicing, inaugurated by his coming face-to-face with life's *duhkha* and grappling with basic existential questions.

The enlightenment experience of Siddhartha Gautama was so powerful and transformative that everyone around him could see the transformation in his way of being. It is said that five wandering ascetics, who had met him both during the period of his search and then right after his enlightenment experience, became his disciples right there and then. His words of guidance and encouragement to all those who sought the way to an enlightened way of life were kept in memory by those who heard them, and came to be written down for posterity.

We now have a voluminous corpus of scriptures called *sutras* (literally "strands" that tie together points of teaching) in which the Buddha's teachings are preserved. Each sutra opens with the phrase "Thus I have heard . . ." indicating that the anonymous writer is simply transmitting the words of the Buddha. These sutras were then supplemented through the ages by numerous commentaries written by thoughtful disciples. Compilations of precepts that regulate a kind of life leading to and issuing forth from enlightenment were also written down in different stages.

The Zen tradition, however, sets itself apart from this publicly accessible written body of teachings, claiming access to Shakyamuni's enlightenment through direct transmission. This transmission is said to have been given in a continuous line beginning with Mahakashyapa. Claimed by the Zen lineage to be the designated successor of Shakyamuni, Mahakashyapa's lineage continued down through Bodhidharma, who then continued the line in China. Through these disciples, the transmission continued through Korean and Japanese Zen masters, and so on to the present time.

The beginning of this direct transmission is described in the following story, included in a famous collection of Zen episodes (koans) entitled *Wu-men Kuan* (in Japanese, *Mumonkan*), or *The Gateless Gate.*[2]

> *Once, in ancient times, when the World-Honored One was giving a sermon at Mt. Grdhakuta, he held up a flower and showed it to the assemblage. At this, they all remained silent. Only the venerable Kashyapa broke into a smile. The World-Honored One said, "I have the eye treasury of the True Dharma, the marvelous mind of nirvana, the true form of no-form, the subtle gate of the Dharma. It does not depend on letters, being specially transmitted outside all teachings. Now I entrust Mahakashyapa with this.*[3]

This anecdote indicates how the Awakened One chose his successor: with direct transmission of his enlightenment and without so many words—in fact, with no words at all.

The Zen program of training involves years of practice in meditation and, in some lineages, *koan* study. During this time, the practitioner has frequent one-to-one encounters with the Zen master and goes through a series of episodes that embody the concrete circumstances in which their various Zen ancestors attained enlightenment.[4] In these sessions with the teacher, practitioners cut through boundaries of time and space and enter into the very mind of each ancestor. One after another, the student "appropriates" the ancestor's enlightenment experience as his or her very own.

This process is imaged as the handing down of a precious elixir from the hands of the master into the disciple's cupped hands—continuing through the ages in a way that never diminishes the source, the enlightenment of Shakyamuni himself.

These episodes depicting the transmissions of the successive lineage holders are largely based on reconstructed accounts of later generations. They aim, in part, to validate the lineages historically. Reenacted in one-to-one encounters between master and disciple, they are significant expressions of the awakened mind of the Zen lineage ancestors.

Mind-to-mind transmission is crucial in maintaining the continuity of a Zen lineage. Such encounters actualize what master Wu-men (the compiler of the *Wu-men Kuan,* or "Gateless Gate") wrote in the thirteenth century:

> . . . *as one experiences the awakening to the true self, one is able to "walk hand-in-hand with the whole descending line of Zen masters and be eyebrow-to-eyebrow with them . . . to see with the same eye that they see with, hear with the same ear that they hear with.*[5]

Looking at the Zen communities that survive throughout the world today, one cannot help but note the institutionalization that has set in. Within some Zen lineages, the oft repeated one-to-one encounters have been dropped altogether, in favor of more formalized, ritualized ways of authorizing succession.

The Zen emphasis on direct transmission could be compared with the notion of apostolic succession in the Christian tradition. The Roman Catholic, Orthodox, and Anglican churches maintain that the authenticity of their message lies in its direct transmission from the first apostles of Jesus Christ. The comparison, however, stops there. The differences between the two kinds of transmission far outweigh this single similarity. What it does indicate is the importance given, in both the Zen and Christian traditions, to returning to the source. The criterion for authenticity in both traditions is the direct connection with one's origins. In Zen, this is the experience of Shakyamuni's enlightenment; in Christianity, it is the original proclamation of the Gospel message handed down from the disciples who walked and shared bread with Jesus the Christ.

Pointing to the Moon

The second cardinal mark of Zen is expressed in the maxim, "not relying on words or letters." The fundamental experience at the heart of Zen, the experience that illuminates one's whole being, could never be adequately expressed in propositional language. Language, in Zen, is like a finger pointing to the moon. If we foolishly get fixed on the finger or caught up trying to analyze it from various angles, we miss "the point" of the pointing. So Zen reminds us not to get stuck on the finger, that is, not to let words and letters become an obstacle to the direct experience of enlightenment.

Anecdotes tell us of Zen monks who, on sudden inspiration, burned all their sutras in literal fulfillment of this second cardinal mark. One such example is that of Te-shan (782–865; Japanese, Tokusan), disciple of Lung-t'an (Ryutan). In Wu-men's collection of koans, he is described as putting a torch to all his sutras and Buddhist commentaries, saying: "Even though we have exhausted abstruse doctrine, it is like placing a hair in vast space. Even though we have learned the vital points of all truths in the world, it is like a drop of water thrown into a big ravine."[6]

We can note with some irony that there is a *considerable* volume of Zen literature, whose basic message is to not rely on words and letters! Among these are anecdotes and exchanges between Zen masters and practitioners, meant to derail the discursive or rational mind. There are also volumes of poetry composed by practitioners trying to give verbal expression to some insight or glimpse into that realm of enlightenment.

Some lineages encourage celebrating such glimpses—when one successfully passes a koan, for instance—in poetry or calligraphy.[7] These are attempts to use words and letters in order precisely to reaffirm the second Zen maxim of "not relying on words or letters." These expressions may teem with allusions to the natural world—birds, flowers, mountains, and rivers—or ordinary things like chopsticks and bowls. But they are hardly expressions based on discursive or rational thinking, nor are they propositional statements seeking to verify or falsify some truth. Instead they invite us to *taste* or *see* or *hear* and experience the world of enlightenment for ourselves.

In the Sanbo Kyodan lineage, where I was privileged to receive my Zen training, those graced with an affirmed experience of *kensho,* or seeing into one's nature, are asked to write a short account and submit it to the Zen master. In reading these accounts of the enlightenment experience of different persons, one notices that they are irreducible to any one kind of expression, but are as diverse as the individuals so confirmed in having come to such an experience.

Some examples are found in *The Three Pillars of Zen* (based on the practice and teaching of the Sanbo Kyodan in Kamakura, edited by Philip Kapleau). A Japanese executive describes a profound experience triggered by the words of thirteenth-century Zen master, Dogen: "I came to realize clearly that Mind is no other than mountains and rivers and the great wide earth, the sun and the moon and the stars."[8]

A retired Japanese government worker comes to his experience and exclaims: "Oh, it is *this!*"[9]

An American schoolteacher awakens one night with a bright "Ha!" and realized "I was enlightened."[10]

A Japanese insurance adjuster writes how it dawned on him: *"There is Nothing to realize!"*[11]

A Canadian Catholic sister—who had practiced with Yamada Roshi for many years and went on to found Zen centers in the Philippines—writes that her experience was triggered by words of Scripture, specifically those of John the Baptist upon his encounter with the Christ: "Therefore this joy of mine is now full" (John 3:29).[12]

These examples show the variety of verbal expressions of the experience confirmed as genuine Zen enlightenment. While the direct experience can never be fully captured in the words used to express it, the words are taken as the proverbial finger pointing beyond itself to the moon—shining in full glory for all of us to behold, if we only take the effort to look.

Certain notions pertaining to the enlightenment experience are the subject of much discussion in philosophical and religious circles. One such is the notion of "emptiness," or *shunyata* in Sanskrit.[13] While this is not the place to pursue this discussion, we can simply note that the term *shunyata* is repeatedly used in the elucidation of the nature of enlightenment. We might recall here Te-shan's remark that "even though we have exhausted abstruse doctrine, it is like placing a hair in vast space . . ."[14] Echoing this notion in a poetic way, my teacher Yamada Roshi often cited his teacher, Hakuun Yasutani, who described this realm of enlightenment in this way: "Not a speck of cloud in the sky, to mar the gazing eye."[15]

These are helpful warnings not to place ultimacy in verbal expressions, but to go deeper than these in delving into the truth of Zen. "Not relying on words or letters," however, can also serve as a convenient excuse for not engaging in the tedious, yet necessary, endeavor to clarify important concepts and to communicate through language. An anti-intellectual tendency has always been present in the Zen tradition. Disdaining the pursuits of analytic mind, this attitude—if persistently and stubbornly maintained—can only be reproved as intellectual indolence.

We need only look at the example of Shakyamuni to see that this indolent attitude of just retreating into silence is a pitfall. After his enlightenment experience, it is said that the Buddha was overwhelmed by its implications, and remained speechless for weeks: the profundity of his realization was beyond all words and letters. And so he remained in that silence for a long time, basking in quiet contemplation of the wondrous realm that was opened to him. He was tempted to remain in that state for the rest of his life, simply relishing the fruits of enlightenment for himself. But he was persuaded by the deva Brahma to share what he saw with his fellow beings, lest it be lost to the world.

Ultimately it was the Buddha's compassion that moved him to take efforts to speak the ineffable, to show others the way to this experience. And from that moment on—using words in a way that pointed beyond themselves—he was ready to expound the inexpressible Dharma to anyone who would listen, adapting his words to the capacity of the listener.

Any attempt to express what is ultimately inexpressible is fraught with self-contradiction. So the Zen tradition emphasizes "not relying on words or letters." Nevertheless we must use language, and use it well, to communicate what we have experienced and know as true with other human beings. Thus the maxim "not relying on words or letters" is self-referential; it tells us to not take it (i.e., the maxim of "not relying on words or letters") as ultimate or absolute truth in itself.

In certain dramatic instances, silence speaks louder than words. There is a famous account of the enlightened layman Vimalakirti engaging in a verbal joust with other disciples of the Buddha, in an attempt to capture the essence of enlightenment in words. The whole episode climaxes with his thunderous silence overcoming the arguments of all the others. Such silence is not just a refusal to use words; it is arrived at when, having gone to the ultimate limits to which words can take us, we exhaust their possibilities.

Words, in Zen, serve mainly as skillful means to point beyond themselves. As there is an express disavowal of the ultimacy of words and letters, orthodoxy or heresy does not become an issue. The issue is *orthopraxis*—meaning it's not what one says or even believes, but what one does. The point, in Zen, is for our life and actions to express the wisdom and compassion of one who has awakened to one's true self.

This opens the possibility for persons of differing religious beliefs to practice genuine Zen. This is the basic stance taken by Yamada Roshi, who welcomed as Zen disciples not only Buddhists, but also Christians, Jews, and those with no particular religious affiliation. He did not require them either to profess nor renounce their religious faith or affiliation, insofar as this did not present anything incompatible with or obstructive to their Zen practice.

When questioned on this, Yamada would respond that in the practice of Zen, the Christian's faith could be purified, enabling the practitioner to become a much better Christian; the Jew, a much better Jew; the Buddhist, a much better Buddhist. He especially invited his Zen disciples who were also practicing Christians—whose numbers kept growing through the years—to express their Christian faith from the perspective of their Zen experience, and conversely, to express their Zen experience from the perspective of their Christian faith. This book is my continuing attempt to respond to this invitation.

Touching the Core of Our Being

The third maxim of Zen is this: Zen points directly to the human mind or heart. These English terms *(mind, heart)* correspond to the Chinese *hsin* or, in Japanese, *kokoro,* which refer to the very core of our being. Zen invites us to an experience at this very core of who we are—an experience that sheds light on every aspect of our lives.

From this core of our being arises the fundamental, life-and-death question we inevitably ask at some point in our lives, in different modalities: Who am I? What is my true self? How am I to understand myself in relation to the entire universe? What is the meaning of all this? How can I live my life fully in a way that I can be at peace in the face of death? What is the one thing necessary in this life?

This is the kind of question the rich young man asked of Jesus: What must I do to attain eternal life? (Mark 10:17 ff.) And it was the question Hui-k'o asked around the sixth century of Bodhidharma, when he was finally granted an audience with the bearded monk from the western regions: "Your disciple's mind is not yet at peace. I beg you, Master, give it rest."[16] These are questions that shake us at the very foundations of our being, coming from the core of who we are.

When we use the term "spiritual," we are referring to this core of our being. *World Spirituality: An Encyclopaedic History of the Religious Quest*, offers this working definition: "The spiritual core is the deepest center of the person. It is here that the person is open to the transcendent dimension. It is here that the person experiences ultimate reality."[17]

The cultivation of *spirituality* thus cuts across the many religious traditions, and adherents of most religions can engage in meaningful conversation with one another when they refer to this dimension of our existence. The spirituality of a religious tradition is the mode of life issuing from the core, as understood and lived in that tradition. Thus Zen spirituality is a synonym for the Zen way of life, as this way of life issues forth from the center of our being.

In the Christian context, the term spirituality comes from the Latin *spiritus,* coming from the verb *spirare,* "to breathe." Spiritual life, life at the core, has something to do with the breath—the *ruah* in Hebrew scriptures, coming as it does from a divine Source (Gen. 1:2). On this significant point, the Jewish and Christian traditions can engage in conversation with Zen.

Zen responds the core question, "Who am I?" by way of an invitation: Look and see! (Seek and you shall find!) Take up the practice, and your eyes will be opened! And what is there to see? The fourth maxim tells us that what we see is our own true nature. And in seeing this, we become an Awakened One (a Buddha).

Seeing One's Nature, Being Awakened

The fourth mark of Zen is seeing into one's very own nature. Seeing what one really is, one becomes an Awakened One; seeing what, or who, one really is, one also sees all things as they really are. This is seeing without distortion or delusion. This is why the Awakened One is said to have realized wisdom in its fullness.

Zen enlightenment opens the eyes of wisdom. The wisdom of an Awakened One is inseparable from compassion, because "seeing things as they really are" is seeing that we are vitally interconnected with one another and with everything else. This is the basis of compassion: *com-passion* means "suffering with," as opposed to mere sympathy or pity toward another being. Seeing our interconnectedness with everything in the universe transforms our way of being, as we become one who shares the pains as well as the joys of all beings. In other words, the joys and sorrows of all beings are realized as one's very own. *Suffering with* and *being joyful with* flow naturally out of being awakened, being a Buddha. Awakening to who we are unleashes the compassion flowing at

the heart of our being. Compassion can then flow into the totality of our life—throwing light into our relationships with our fellow humans, and with the Earth as a whole.

In Zen, opening the eyes of wisdom in the enlightenment
experience overcomes our dysfunctional mode of being, characterized by alienation from the natural world, from fellow human
beings, and from our true selves. Thus opening the eyes of wisdom leads to the recovery of our wholeness.

These four marks, or cardinal principles of Zen, indicate the
dynamic and living character of Zen spirituality. Let us now consider its fruits as they come to bear in our life.

Three Fruits of the Zen Life

The fulcrum of Zen is the practice of seated meditation *(zazen)*.
This practice enables three fruits to come to bear in one's life: (1)
the deepening of one's power of concentration *(joriki)*; (2) the
awakening to one's true nature *(kensho)*; and (3) the actualization
of the way of enlightenment in one's daily life *(mujodo no taigen,*
literally, "embodiment of the supreme way").[18]

Concentration

The first fruit, *concentration,* does not mean what we ordinarily
associate with the word. Imagine, for example, Rodin's sculpture
"The Thinker," with his right elbow on his right knee and his
clenched hand raised to support his head, as if concentrating on
some thought or other. This posture shows a person caught up in
something. It indicates a state of mind wherein the thinker is distinct from the thought; the subject is distinct from the object.
This is exactly the opposite of Zen.

As long as we remain in a state of mind characterized by that
subject-object dichotomy, we remain in a state of ordinary

consciousness with "I" (ego) at the center and everything revolving around it. Everything we encounter in our life-world—including all other persons and living beings—remain as objects confronting a subject (myself). Thus even the notion of God becomes relegated to an object "out there."

In the Zen context, *con-centration* is a state of mind and being where the separation between subject and object is overcome. In this state we are focused at and grounded in the core of our being, where we find our true home. The key term here, *con-centration*, indicates coming-together with the *center* of one's being. We could also call this a state of integration, of wholeness. Here all aspects of our being find their proper place in a unified totality. As our con-centration deepens, the disparate elements of our life come together, and we experience a sense of wholeness and harmony.

This is the power of "single-minded attention" (*joriki* in Japanese). We are fully present in the here and now, in everything we do. Present for the fullness each moment, we can respond fully with our whole being to the call of each situation. Distracting thoughts, extrinsic forces, and inordinate attachments do not detract from this core of our being. In such a state of con-centration, we live each moment—each thought, word, action, event, or encounter in our daily life—to the fullest.

The most effective way to come to this state is through the practice of seated meditation. In this practice, we intentionally place our whole being in the here and now by being attentive to, becoming one with, each breath. As we become more familiar with this way of being aware in the here and now, this kind of awareness naturally flows over into our daily life—whether we're engaged in activities or are in a state of quiet relaxation.

Seeing into One's True Nature

As one goes on in Zen practice, the power of con-centration deepens from day to day. There may then come a moment—during zazen or, more likely, at some unguarded moment in daily life—when a sudden flash occurs. And in this moment we glimpse a dimension that entirely transforms our whole way of seeing and being.

This experience is called "seeing into one's true nature" (ken-sho). It is the turning point in the life of Zen. We will simply describe this experience briefly here and address it in greater detail in Chapter 4.[19]

Although referred to as a "fruit" of Zen practice, kensho is perhaps more properly described as a gift, a touch of grace (to use the Christian phrase). We are readied to receive this gift by the effort we put into our practice of meditation, whereby we rid ourselves of all those things that block it from being fully manifest in our lives. The intentionality with which we bring our attention fully to every moment enables us to be constantly vigilant, ready and open to receive the gift.

The obstacles to the experience of kensho are due to our own self-centered attitudes and ways of thinking and behaving. Our own egocentric attachments and tendencies pulling us in different directions, our very desire to be in control, all make it impossible to listen with our whole being to that primal wordless Word which is addressing us at every moment.

The definitive moment may come during meditation when our mind is still and fully attentive. Or it may come in some idle moment in daily life. In a flash, the universe may break open for us and allow us to see things as they really are. This momentous event could be triggered by the chirp of a bird, the sound of a bell, someone's sneeze, a tap on the shoulder. It could even be a mental image, thought, or memory. Whatever triggers it, the glimpse is clear and unmistakable—and in that moment, we are ushered into a whole new world.

At the same time, we see that it's the same old world we've been in all along. But now we're surprised to see it in an entirely different light—with a sense of "Why didn't I see this before?" In the kensho experience, like a clear day in the noonday sun, everything stands out in full splendor and glory.

Zen master Dogen described two ways of seeing—one based on delusion, the other on an awakened perspective—like this: "Putting oneself forth seeing myriad things is delusion. Myriad things coming forth seeing the self is enlightenment."[20]

The initial experience of awakening can have a stunning emotional impact. Accompanied by great joy and a sense of exhilaration and liberation, one may also be moved to laughter or to tears, or both. The emotional effect can remain for hours or even days—perhaps making the person experiencing it seem like one has gone off the deep end.

When the emotional excitement and spectacular effects of the initial enlightenment experience subside, we reach a plateau of calmness and serenity, a quiet yet unmistakable kind of joy. We come back to the ordinariness of everyday life, but with one crucial difference: we now are able to see through the delusions of the egoic self that prevented us from seeing things as they are.

The third fruit of Zen practice is the actualization of this initial glimpse and a gradual realization of its implications in daily life.

Embodying the Peerless Way

Having once seen into our true nature, having glimpsed that vast, immeasurable, indescribable realm that constitutes one's true self, it becomes all the more important to continue Zen practice. We can thus bring this experience to fruition in our life—and it won't simply become something wonderful that happened in the past.

Continued practice also enables us to prevent *Zen sickness* from taking hold of us. This is a state of mind that—given the power and impact of that glimpse of the world of enlightenment—becomes fixated on the enthralling, fascinating, or startling visions we may have experienced in that flash of realization. Attachment to these emotional effects, or longing for their return, can consume us and make us lose our balance and perspective. Practice enables us to overcome any "sickness-causing" tendencies. So our glimpse of the world of the true self can become part of our everyday life, and bear fruit in it.

Zen practice then becomes simply "letting things be" as they really are. Every facet of life finds its concrete place in this light. This level of practice could be described as "basking in the miracle of ordinariness." Zen masters describe it wonderfully: "When hungry, eat; when thirsty, take a drink; when sleepy, go to sleep." This is a life in total harmony with one's true nature, an authentic way of living one's life.

Now, if Zen is just about eating when hungry, drinking when thirsty, sleeping when sleepy, what is the difference between life after awakening and any other life? The answer is *no* difference—and all the difference in the world.

There is no difference because the Zen practitioner eats, drinks, and sleeps like anyone. But the awakened person is no longer deluded by a false ego that says "I" eat, "I" drink, "I" go to sleep, and so on. Without the deluded perspective of "I," one is no longer swayed by its inordinate desires or divisive designs. That "I" has been seen through—and realized to be empty, to be no-thing.

In Christian terms, when we partake in ordinary human activities with awakened eyes, our eating, drinking, sleeping, laughing, crying could be said to fully manifest the purity of divine grace. With awakened eyes, we see the miracle of ordinariness in daily life, replete with a sense of mystery. And with a deep-felt gratitude for everything, we experience it as *nothing but* the pure grace that comes from a divine source.

When we awaken to the true nature of things, we also see through the false separation of subject and object, the "I" opposed to "Other." In other words, we see the interconnectedness of all things. I am what I am *because* everything else in the universe is what it is; everything else in this universe is what it is because I am who I am.

This is the ground of the natural outflow of compassion. If no one in the universe is separate from me, I realize that my neighbor's joy and sorrow are *my* joy and sorrow. "Being-with" and "suffering-with" characterize a life of compassion, and become our fundamental mode of being, day in and day out. From now on, it's a matter of steeping ourselves more deeply in an awareness of interconnectedness. Then every facet of our life will be penetrated and transformed by this awareness. This deepening awareness is the third fruit of Zen: embodying the peerless way in our ordinary life.

With this description of the four cardinal marks, and more notably, of the three fruits of the Zen way of life, we have offered our response to the question "What is Zen?" The response, summarizing all the above, is simply this: "You will know it by its fruits."

Now, step-by-step, we can consider how such a way of life leads to the healing of our broken humanity and our wounded Earth. For this, we will look more closely at the threefold fruit of the Zen life.

The third chapter focuses on the first fruit of Zen practice, *deepening con-centration,* and the art of listening to the breath. The fourth chapter looks at the second fruit, *the experience of awakening,* and the implications of true selfhood for healing. The fifth and sixth chapters deal with the third fruit, *embodying the peerless way* in daily life—and its implications for healing our own woundedness and that of the entire Earth.

3

Listening to the Breath

ZEN CAN BE described as the art of living in attunement with the Breath. In this chapter, we will consider the concrete elements of Zen practice, in light of the first of the fruits of Zen. What is offered is somewhat by way of a recipe, with additional explanation of its various ingredients. The actual cooking and, of course, the eating is up the reader. So be prepared to put down the book, buckle down to practice, and let the living Breath of Zen lead the way.

This is an important point. Reading books on spirituality or religious themes, in general, may leave us feeling uplifted or inspired. But if we let it go at that, this nice, fuzzy feeling won't last. We will soon we need a boost from the next book.

A recipe has inherent limitations as reading material. At most, it can whet the appetite; it cannot provide the nourishment we seek. The proof of a recipe, like the proverbial pudding, is in the eating.

Elements of Zen Practice

To begin the practice of Zen, three elements are set in place. First, we take a posture conducive to the practice. Second, we become aware of our breathing. And, third, we quiet the mind to the point of stillness.

A Conducive Posture

Six possible positions are recommended for sitting meditation, or *zazen*. To help keep the back straight in any of these positions, it is helpful to imagine a straight line running from the ceiling down through one's head and backbone.

1. In full lotus the legs are folded, with the right foot on the left thigh and the left foot on the right thigh, as one sits on a pillow or round cushion. This is the most desirable meditation position, as we can sit completely balanced, with a straight back.

2. For those who can't manage full lotus, the half-lotus is next best position. Sit with the left foot on right thigh and right foot under the left thigh; or vice versa, with right foot on left thigh and left foot under the right thigh. Again, one sits on an uplifted cushion that lets the knees touch and be firmly based on the mat or floor.

3. For those whose bone structure doesn't allow the legs to bend in full or half-lotus position, the so-called Burmese position is recommended. Sitting on a cushion, the left foot is tucked under the right thigh, and the right foot under the left thigh. It does not matter which is above the other.

4. For those who cannot sit in any of these three ways, a prayer stool is recommended. Sitting with one's legs under the stool enables one to keep a straight back.

5. A fifth way is to sit with one's buttocks placed—with or without a cushion or padding—over the cupped heels. This is the formal seated position called *seiza* in Japanese.
6. Using a low chair or stool, sit on the front part of the chair without leaning back, and keep one's back straight.

The hands are placed lightly above the thighs, left palm over right palm, with the thumbs touching slightly to make an oval shape with the entire hand position.

In the two schools of Zen that prevailed in Japan—the *Rinzai* (Chinese, Lin-chi) and the *Soto* (Chinese, *T'sao-tung*) schools—there are some differences in sitting styles. Rinzai practitioners sit facing one another; those of the Soto school sit facing the wall. In my own experience, the advantage of facing a wall is that it minimizes distraction.

In either case, the eyes are kept slightly open, with the line of sight about one yard ahead or at the lower part of the wall one faces. Without staring, let the eyes simply rest on one point.

There are several advantages to having one's eyes slightly open. Closing the eyes makes one more susceptible to either drowsiness or the barrage of images unrelated to practice. Open eyes keeps us attentive to the here and now, not to a world of one's own imagining. More importantly, open eyes keep the sense of the interconnectedness, or non-separation, of the "I" and what surrounds it.

While formal Zen practice is done in sitting meditation, or *zazen*, this is not all there is to Zen. All possible human postures taken in our daily ordinary life are expressions of Zen—and meant to be integrated into the life of Zen.

East Asian tradition describes four human postures, including: *gyo* (literally, "going"), the human being in action, such as walking, running, or engaging in some kind of physical activity; *ju* (literally, "dwelling" or "remaining"), a stance of passivity, such as simply standing at attention; *za* (literally, "seated") a seated posture described above; and *ga* (literally, "prostrate") the posture of lying down to rest or sleep. In all four of these human postures, we are called to be fully aware of the here and now.

In Western spiritual traditions, posture is not a major consideration in meditation or contemplative prayer. Of course, we see pictures of saints or religious persons kneeling in prayer; and human beings seem to take this posture in the presence of the divine. This comes perhaps from a cultural context where bending one's knees before a higher authority is a commonly acknowledged sign of submission and respect. Note, for example, Paul's comment in the letter to the Philippians: "At the name of Jesus, every knee should bow, in heaven and on earth and under the earth . . ." (Phil. 2:10).

We can only speculate about the posture Jesus may have taken in his own prayer. Based on artists' conceptions, we see him kneeling with hands folded or almost prostrate, as in the agony in the Garden of Gethsemane. Christians normally take a standing position when saying the "prayer of Jesus," the Our Father, or sit on benches or church pews when not using kneelers, in a common posture in prayer.

In his *Spiritual Exercises,* St. Ignatius of Loyola describes the different possibilities of posture for meditation or contemplation. These include not only kneeling, but also standing, sitting, walking, or being prostrate, supine, and so forth. In his "Additional Directions for the First Week of the Exercises," he notes:

> *I will enter into the meditation, at times kneeling, at times prostrate on the ground, at other times supine, or seated or standing, always intent on seeking what I desire. After I have finished an Exercise I will examine for the space of a quarter of an hour, either while sitting or walking, how I have succeeded in the meditation or contemplation.*[1]

By contrast, Zen is more directive regarding posture. When one finds a suitable seated posture for meditation, one is ready to turn to the second element, attention to the breath.

Following the Breath

The breath is generally not attended to in most Western writings on meditation or contemplative practice—with some exceptions. The *Philokalia,* for example, contains this passage:

> *You know, brother, how we breathe; we breathe the air in and out. On this is based the life of the body and on this depends its warmth. So, sitting down in your cell, collect your mind, lead it to the path of the breath along which the air enters in, constrain it to enter the heart altogether with the inhaled air, and keep it there. Keep it there, but do not leave it silent and idle; instead, give it the following prayer: "Lord, Jesus Christ, Son of God, have mercy upon me." Let this be its constant occupation, never to be abandoned. For this work, by keeping the mind free from dreaming, renders it unassailable to suggestions of the enemy and leads it to Divine desire and love.*[2]

St. Ignatius gives a concrete description of one form of prayer through breathing. In his third method of prayer, he recommends that "at each breath or respiration, (the exercitant) is to pray mentally, silently saying one word of the *Our Father,* or any other familiar prayer, so that between one breath and another, a single word is said."[3]

The recitation of a single word of a well-known prayer with every breath immerses the practitioner in the atmosphere (literally "the sphere of the breath") of divine presence, integrating the prayer not just mentally but with one's whole body.

St. John of the Cross also experienced the significance of breathing and contemplative prayer. As he writes in his *Spiritual Canticle:*

> The breathing of the air is properly of the Holy Spirit, for which the soul here prays, so that she may love God perfectly. She calls it the breathing of the air, because it is a most delicate touch and feeling of love which habitually in this state is caused in the soul by the communion of the Holy Spirit. Breathing with His Divine Breath, He raises the soul most sublimely, and informs her that she may breathe in God the same breath of love that the Father breathes in the Son, and the Son in the Father, which is the same Holy Spirit that they breathe into her in the said transformation. And this is for the soul so high a glory, and so profound and sublime a delight, that it cannot be described by mortal tongue, nor can human understanding, as such, attain to any conception of it.[4]

In Zen meditation, the breath is the fulcrum of our practice. The breath brings us in touch with the very core of our being: a mysterious and marvelous source of power and healing. Because most of us have actually forgotten how to breathe, we have lost touch with this living core. By enabling us to recover the art of breathing naturally, Zen practice enables us to be at home and at peace with ourselves.

In my mother tongue, Tagalog, the word *pahinga* means "to let breathe"; it also means "to rest" or "repose." Zen masters point out that the most natural way to breathe is like a sleeping newborn baby. Its whole being is given over to each breath in a most natural way—a way that we have to relearn as adults.

In sitting meditation, maintaining a straight back enables us to breathe naturally. For those just beginning Zen meditation practice, it is helpful to count the breaths: "one" on the in-breath, "two" on the out-breath, and so on up to ten. Then start again. Simply resume counting each time you notice your mind wanders away from this counting. By focusing on each breath, we are able to harness the mind. This is like making use of a walking stick to help us along when we feel weak and wobbly. Or, to take an image from the Philippine countryside, it's like carving successive notches on the trunk of a coconut tree; these foot-holds help us climb the tree.

As we become accustomed to harnessing the mind to the breath, the counting is modified. We could then count only the out-breaths, from one to ten and back to one; then, count up to three and back to one; and then just "one," repeatedly.

The counting of the breath is not a mere mechanical activity. With each breath, it invites the practitioner to experience the fullness of the here and now. In this way, we can come to a deep experience of stillness and oneness.

I recall directing a weekend Zen retreat for a group of senior high school students, who were all new to this practice. After initiating them in the preliminaries, I recommended breath-counting for the entire weekend period. Most of them spent their time on this exercise, as directed. At the end of the retreat, the participants were gathered and invited, over tea, to share their experience. As expected, many recounted initial difficulties with posture or with adjusting to the rigorous schedule.

But one student, who had had her share of leg and back pains, shared how, throughout all this, she remained faithful to her counting. Then in one brief moment, she lost herself and became absorbed in just one breath: she "became one with the number *three*." This landmark moment gave her a taste of something entirely new. A moment of oneness with the number *three* (it could have been *one*, *two*, or *ten*) was a veritable moment of grace. That made all the difference in her appreciation of the practice. For her, Zen was no longer just a rigorous exercise of leg-folding and breath-counting. Becoming "one with the number *three*" gave her a glimpse of the world of inner freedom and interconnectedness.

When counting the breath becomes easier, we can forego the numbers altogether. Simply follow the breath with the mind—in and out—as you inhale and exhale. This is like being able to climb more agilely up and down the coconut tree, without aid of the notches on the trunk.

Other types of Eastern meditation have detailed instructions for breathing and prescriptions for breathing exercises. In Hatha Yoga, for example, one nostril is blocked with the finger while breathing in through the other nostril; then that nostril is blocked, while exhaling through the other. Such exercises help to heighten awareness of the breath, and they may be adapted to our own preparations for practice. But they are not normally employed in Zen practice, except as prescriptions for those individuals with breathing difficulties.

The prescribed way to breathe in Zen is normally and naturally—and deeply, centered on the lower diaphragm, or *hara* in Japanese. Our whole heart and mind is placed on each breath as it comes in and goes out. So each breath is fresh, lived in each here and now. This living in the here and now, guided by the breath, opens us to a deeper level of awareness.

Silencing the Mind

When we can bring our attention to the breath, the third point in the practice of seated meditation takes care of itself: allowing the mind to become silent.

This third point is actually the most difficult to accomplish and most troublesome to deal with, requiring a great deal of struggle.

Anyone who tries to sit still for a few seconds will find that the mind naturally tends to wander to one thought after another.

That is simply the way it works in our ordinary consciousness: mind actively pursues objects of thought for reflection or rumination. Zen practice invites us to regulate this mental activity—using breath-counting as one very effective way to do this—thus helping this normally discursive, restless mind to become still in the here and now.

How does one deal with stray thoughts? This is the most common question asked by meditators. In Zen meditation, the rule of thumb is this: Neither pursue them nor forcefully drive them away. By pursuing or engaging in thoughts, we separate ourselves from the here and now. When we forcefully drive them away, they come back with a vengeance. The most effective way to deal with discursive thoughts is to simply recognize them as such; then, go back to the breath.

In some forms of Eastern meditation, *mantra* is employed to focus the mind. This is a word or short phrase given by the meditation master to the practitioner, who will then recite it during meditation. Thus mantra becomes a focal point, around which the practitioner can rally. This mitigates the entry of discursive thoughts, while keeping the mind focused. Some Christian spiritual directors have adapted mantra—choosing the Holy Name or a word or phrase from Sacred Scriptures that strikes a resonating chord—to still the mind in meditation or contemplation.

A helpful hint on this point was given by the late Fr. Hugo Enomiya-Lassalle, S.J., one of the first Christians to go deeply into Zen. After over thirty years of practice—and in his eighties—he was given permission to teach Zen, by his teacher, Yamada Roshi.[5] In the Zen retreats he directed in Europe and Japan, he repeatedly told practitioners to deal with stray thoughts "as Mt. Fuji would deal with the clouds that come its way." Just as the mountain is in no way affected by passing clouds, remain there unmoved and unperturbed.

This is the marvelous simplicity at the very heart of Zen. Known in Japanese as *shikan taza* (from Zen master Dogen), it literally means "just sitting." We will go further into "single-minded sitting" in the next chapter.

In the Rinzai school of Zen, as also in the Sanbo Kyodan lineage, a device known as a *koan* is used to cut through mind's discursive activity by forcing it to a corner from which it cannot free itself using rationality. A particular koan may serve as a mantra, such as the famous *mu* koan. More about mu and koan practice is explained in the next chapter. Suffice it to say, here, that koans are employed to silence the restless mind by putting a stop to discursiveness.

Koan practice cannot be taken up on one's own. It must be done under the continuing direction of an authorized Zen teacher, who has gone through the koan practice herself or himself. Otherwise it is easy to be misled by koan practice; construing all kinds of answers suggested by the many readily available books on Zen, we miss the mark entirely.

The Zen Teacher as Midwife

In Zen practice, one cannot emphasize enough the vital role of the teacher, someone who has made this arduous journey to the core and is familiar with the terrain. No amount of Zen literature can take the place of guidance from an authentic Zen teacher.

A source of greatest blessing in my own life was to have been sent to Japan as a Jesuit student in my early twenties, in 1970. The school where I was sent to learn Japanese language was located in Kamakura, about an hour's train ride from Tokyo. Here, too, the San-un Zendo, the Zen Hall of the Three Clouds, is located. And here I had the privilege of being initiated into Zen by Yamada Roshi. Guided by his astute hand and compassionate heart, I was led step-by-step into the world of Zen, finishing formal koan training under his direction in 1988.

There is so much I would like to express about this journey to the inner world of Zen, guided by Yamada Roshi. But this will have to wait. For now, I can only express my gratitude for this privilege by carrying out the mandate I received to carry on the tradition and, by virtue of this, to assist others who wish to undertake the same journey.

One of my greatest joys over the years has been helping out in Zen retreats. Enabled to let go of their baggage, participants come to a fundamental experience of "seeing into one's true nature." The feeling one gets assisting in this process is that of a midwife assisting in the birthing of a new life. The midwife is by no means the source of that life, but simply sees to it that the way is cleared and conditions made favorable for a new life to see the light. And each birth is a joyous and exciting event, filled with wonder and mystery.

The Zen teacher-disciple relationship is a covenant, whereby the teacher agrees to render to the disciple whatever is called for for that disciple to more fully live a life of oneness and interconnectedness. In turn, the disciple looks to the teacher for guidance on this vital journey into the mystery of Being. It is understood that the disciple will take this teacher's word to be authoritative in matters relating to Zen practice and, while in this covenant, will not turn to other teachers for help on similar matters.

Especially for beginners, to go from teacher to teacher may only be confusing; teachers inevitably have different styles and there may be conflicting points in the details of practice. To avoid such confusion, it is important to follow the guidance of *one* teacher in whom one has confidence.

If, however, one begins to feel that a particular teacher is not best suited for oneself, one is always free to express this, bid farewell, and go to a teacher with whom one feels a better resonance. This is not a breaking of the covenant; it is a conclusion of the covenant. And it enjoins the student to set aside and forget everything received from the former teacher. Then nothing stands in the way of the guidance of the new teacher.

A true teacher makes no issue of a disciple's departure. Wishing only the practitioner's greater good, he or she is ready to help the student find someone else. The guiding principle for the teacher is a famous Japanese proverb, *Kuru mono wo kobamazu, saru mono wo owazu,* "not refusing those who come, not pursuing those who go."

The fundamental steps of Zen meditation described in this chapter can in no way take the place of a living teacher. This is only an outline of the practice for those of you who wish to begin on your own. Then you will need a suitable teacher to direct you toward greater depths.

It is hoped, however, that this will whet your appetite for a greater awareness of the mystery of Being. But better than following the instructions in the cookbook, seek an experienced chef, like a mother or aunt or grandmother, who can show you just how to put the ingredients together and point out little things that make all the difference in the taste of the final dish.

Ultimately, the task of the Zen teacher is to help the practitioner be fully tamed, healed, and transformed by the power of the Breath. One definition of Zen is simply "the art of living in attunement with the Breath." And, ultimately, the Breath itself will be the most reliable guide on your journey.

In the Christian tradition, the spiritual director also plays an important role in the deepening of an individual's spiritual development and practice of authentic Christian living. The priest-confessor is the traditional role model of someone the faithful could relate to as an authorized representative of the Christian community. The confessor also serves as a confidante in matters of conscience and a guide for the spiritual journey.

The role of spiritual director can also be taken by persons who are not necessarily ordained in the church. They could be individuals who are graced with the gift of being able to listen and to be for others something like a mirror, in which they can see themselves and their own souls more clearly.

And it is a precious gift to be friends with someone who can be our spiritual confidante. Although not like a spiritual director in the formal sense, the sharing of our spiritual life with another can help us see some things more clearly than when we keep them to ourselves.

The role of a spiritual director is especially crucial for progress in meditation and contemplative prayer. In the *Spiritual Exercises* of St. Ignatius, for example, a director must be well versed in these exercises, especially when helping with the very delicate endeavor called "discernment of spirits." This asks us to look into the movements within, to discern if they originate from a divine source—and therefore need to be ascertained and given heed to— or from another source that must be shunned. This kind of discernment is crucial in making decisions that affect our way of life and our way of dealing with others.

Rediscovering the Breath

Most of us living in this fast-paced contemporary society have actually forgotten how to breathe. Not that we don't perform the biological function, taking in the gases that sustain our life and exhaling what we don't need. But this is done largely unconsciously. We maintain ourselves without being aware of it. For most of us, this biological function is taken for granted.

One of my earliest memories is going with my mother to a funeral service held at a house near ours, in my hometown in the Philippines. My mother held me by the hand as we lined up in the living room parlor to pay our last respects to the deceased, a distant uncle whom I did not recall very well. Beside the coffin, I was lifted up and made to look very closely at the face of the deceased. That early face-to-face encounter with death left a deep impression upon me.

Later, as we were walking home hand-in-hand, I asked my mother: "*Inay* (mother in Tagalog), why do people die?" And I clearly recall how Mother answered me without batting an eye: "That's because they forget to breathe." This answer left me worried. I took a deep breath or two right then, to make sure I didn't forget; and I couldn't sleep that night, anxious that I might forget to breathe in my sleep.

This early childhood memory is a landmark on my journey toward an awareness of the breath and its transformative and healing power. Years later in Japan, when I began my Zen practice under an authentic Zen master, this awareness was taken to a new level.

Through the three-pointed practice of zazen—posture, breathing, and mind-quieting—we are naturally led to a deeper familiarity with the workings of the breath in our life. As we go about our day to day activities, for example, the pace of our breathing varies: shallow and hurried when we become flustered, a great sigh of relief when we finish a task or overcome some difficulty. Our breathing changes with different states of mind. When we pay no attention to our breathing, we easily get dispersed in many directions, feeling a lack of cohesion in our life.

In seated meditation, with our back straight, we become aware that breathing—naturally but deeply, intentionally, slow, and centered on the lower diaphragm—is not just in the lungs. We breathe with our whole body. And as one becomes more and more familiarized with this way of breathing while doing zazen, this way of real-izing one's connectedness with the breath flows into what one does after zazen. One finds oneself breathing more easily and with a greater sense of relaxation and satisfaction.

This process of familiarization with the breath is what we experience as we go on in our practice: the connection between our zazen and the rest of our daily life, taking the fourfold posture given above, *gyo-zen,* or Zen in action, *ju-zen,* or Zen in passivity or relaxation, *ga-zen,* or Zen in horizontal position, that is, even while one is asleep, in addition to *zazen,* comes to be realized more and more.

One helpful way of enhancing this awareness of the connection is by taking advantage of those idle moments in our day, such as while waiting for a red light to turn green at an intersection, while waiting for an appointment, or in the interval that naturally takes place as one goes from one task to another. During those moments, one can intentionally take a deep breath or two, placing oneself in the here and now where one is. As one is able to catch those moments and bring them back to the here and now with the help of the breath, one actually notices the qualitative difference in the way one lives one's day. Instead of losing those moments fidgeting or getting impatient or anxious, one finds that those moments become connectors that tie one's life together, back to the living center where it originates—the here and now.

The Breath as Connector and Healer

One of many motivations that might lead us to Zen practice is an acute need to put together the disparate, or disintegrating, elements of our lives. Simply sitting still—fully relaxed and with no external forces driving us to perform or "do"—we can simply be. In that stillness, we can rediscover the sense of wholeness we are looking for.

Some may ask how this practice of withdrawing from activity and just sitting still can be anything but an escape: Aren't we simply shutting out the world, seeking temporary tranquillity without really making any changes in our life? Isn't such a practice just a form of self-hypnosis, a self-induced euphoric state allowing us to cop-out from the real concerns of the world?

To such questions we can only say that, by sitting in the stillness of zazen, we are focusing our whole being in the here and now. Rather than shutting ourselves off from the rest of the world, we are plunging into the heart of the world. With every breath, we are tuning in to the vital core, tuning in our "receiver," so to speak, to our connectedness with the living universe. Our focus on breathing in and out literally connects us with our own living core and with all living beings—all the human, animal, and plant domains—with whom we share this breath.

By entrusting our being to the Breath, moment to moment, we live in the heart of this circle of interconnectedness. We see our actual connectedness with the oak tree in the garden,[6] and with the Amazon forests, and all the nurturing green plants in the world. We don't even need to keep these images in mind as we breathe; they are already contained in every breath we take.

As our practice deepens and we become more transparent to ourselves, we deepen our awareness of our many unhealed wounds—wounds of unsettled issues, of broken relationships—as well as the wounds of others and of Earth. And the balm that can heal all of these wounds, here and now, lies in each breath we breathe.

Picture a mother gently blowing her warm breath on a child's wounded knee and, in some mysterious but discernible way, healing the child in the process. In the same way, when we entrust our lives to the breath in zazen, we can actually sense that mother's breath on the wounds of our being—and on the wounds of Earth itself. The eyes of the heart open, and the powerful compassion working within and through us pours out toward all sentient beings with whom we share that breath.

The Breath in Christian Spirituality

On a personal note, as I gradually came to a deeper awareness and appreciation of the breath in my life, my reading of the Hebrew Bible and Christian Scriptures took on some fresh perspectives.

For example, the opening lines of the *Book of Genesis* introduce the divine Breath *(ruah)* that lies at the basis of all being and all life, that power which gives everything its form and shape. "In the beginning God created the heavens and the earth. Earth was without form and void, and darkness was upon the face of the deep, and the Breath of God was moving over the face of the waters." (Gen. 1:1–2).

With an awareness of the concrete centrality of breathing in our life, this passage is no longer abstract; it is no longer a subject of theological speculation on the level of concepts. We can see this Breath flowing through us, giving us life and making us what we are. Just as, in the beginning, it moved over the face of the waters, giving everything its form and shape, it now flows through me and the whole universe.

This Breath is the power that inspired the prophets to speak the word of God, uniting the community under God's covenant and calling people to repentance when they strayed from God's path. In the New Testament, the centrality of this Breath in the life of Jesus manifests from the events leading up to his birth, until his final moments on the cross.

John the Baptist, for example, who prepared the way for Jesus' coming and the people's reception of his message, is said to be "filled with the Breath of the Holy One, even from his mother's womb" (Luke 1:15).

Mary, mother of Jesus, is told of the news of his conception with the words: "The Breath of the Holy One will come upon you, and the power of the Most High will cast a shadow over you. Thus the child to be born of you will be Holy and will be called the child of God" (Luke 1:35).

As Jesus comes to adulthood and prepares for his ministry, he is led by the Breath into the desert for forty days (Luke 4:1). Then, purified and confirmed in his mission, he comes back to Galilee in the power of the same Breath (Luke 4:14). Entering a synagogue, he stands before the community and, with the words of the prophet Isaiah, inaugurates his public ministry: "The Breath of the Lord is upon me . . . to preach the Good News to the poor, . . . to proclaim the release of captives, and sight to those who cannot see, to liberate those who are oppressed, and to announce the time of grace of the Lord" (Luke 4:18).

This is the Breath that empowers the life and mission of Jesus. This is the Breath that is in all that he is and does, right up to the final moment on the cross when, having fulfilled his task on earth, he cries out in a loud voice to God: "Into Thy hands, I entrust my Breath" (Luke 24:46).

This is the same Breath that empowers his disciples, transforming them from cowardly, fearful individuals ready to retreat to their fishing nets at the time of Jesus' death, to audacious and confident proclaimers of the Good News of Jesus the Christ, to the ends of the earth.

At Pentecost, this same Breath is poured upon the community of followers, the early Church. The same Breath that empowered Jesus now empowers his followers to witness what he stood for and to proclaim the coming reign of God in Jesus' name to the world. To be a Christian is to be a member of that community of followers of Jesus Christ that is the church. It is to open one's whole life to that very same Breath and be transformed and empowered by it. It is to accept as one's own the mission of Jesus, himself: bearing witnessing to the Good News to all throughout all one's life.

Christian spirituality is literally a life led in the Spirit, or Breath, of Jesus Christ. It is letting this Breath assume centrality in one's being and living a life that "puts on the very mind of Christ" in all that one does.

Zen practice brings all this from an abstract, conceptual theological plane down to a very concrete, experiential level. It deepens our awareness and intimacy with the Breath in day-to-day life. As we live lives fully attuned with the Breath, it becomes the guiding power in our lives. We then experience the gift of healing. And, in our own small ways, each of us is empowered to become an instrument of this Breath in its work of healing a wounded Earth.

4

Awakening to True Self

SOME PEOPLE come to Zen out of curiosity; some are invited by a friend they could not readily refuse. And then there are those who practice Zen for the physical benefits it can bring about: better posture, better circulation, reduction of cholesterol, and so on. And, indeed, it has been medically shown that meditation generally does have such benefits. And needless to say, breathing deeply and naturally and quieting the troubled mind does reduce tension and stress and bring about a sense of inner peace.[1]

Those of us working with the tasks of social and ecological transformation know how demanding such a commitment is. Now and then, we need to step back from our activities and give ourselves some time for silence and reflection. Such a respite allows us to take stock of what we are doing and the directions we're going in. It also allows us to touch base with our spiritual resources, so they can continue to nourish us in these manifold tasks. For the socially and ecologically engaged, Zen practice can provide the "breathing space" and inner nourishment we need to continue.

These are all valid starting points for beginning Zen practice. But whatever our initial motivation is, Zen brings certain fundamental questions to bear in our practice.

The Fundamental Questions

At some point in our lives, we come face-to-face with questions that strike at the core of our being. They may hit in our teens, when all our possibilities ahead of us, or in our twenties when we're faced with career decisions as we try to take stock of our life.

They may hit us when we are well along in life. Or they may hit as a mid-life crisis, putting into doubt or even overturning everything we've established; or as we face the prospect of our own death. We ask ourselves: "What's the point?" "What is this life all about?" "Who am I?" Or, more pragmatically, "What am I living for?" Faced with numerous possibilities, we may ask, "What is the most important thing in life?" A person in search of personal healing may ask: "Where will I find the source of power that can effect my own healing?" While someone working in the social and ecological arenas may say: "How can I get in touch with that source of power that not only heals me, but also nourishes my work in the world?"

And when we begin to see through the egoic self and the six degrees of separation this creates in our being (see Chapter 1, in the section "Tracing the Roots of Our Brokenness"), we may ask: "How can I overcome this inadequate, one-sided image of myself and realize my true self?" In other words, "How can I arrive at true peace of mind, peace within myself, peace with the universe?"

These fundamental questions take us to the crux of Zen. No matter how they're phrased, they cut to the core of our being. We are not seeking a temporary feeling of calm, arrived at by shutting ourselves off from the turmoil of the world, but true inner peace, the kind that lasts. When these are the kind of questions that lead us to Zen, the Zen master knows that we are ready to launch into the deep.

Zen offers two modes of practice for dealing with such fundamental questions. As mentioned above: one mode is *koan* practice; the other is *shikan taza* in Japanese, which means "just sitting," "single-minded sitting." They are the two most effective ways for an individual to actually discover his or her own true self.

The Koan Mu

A *koan* usually consists of an anecdote or episode—in most cases between a monk and an enlightened Zen master—that cuts through the discursive intellect and thus invites us to directly experience our being at its core.

Koan practice is not given to practitioners who are merely interested in the physical, psychological, or intellectual benefits of Zen; it is given to those who are grappling with fundamental issues of human existence. Koan practice is a powerful and direct way to work with and resolve these questions—not in a theoretical or conceptual way, but in a liberating and transformative experience of awakening.

When the master deems we're ready to work with a koan, we are given one that suits our temperament or state of mind. Then in each private interview with the teacher, we demonstrate our grasp of the koan or our experience of it in practice.

There are many koans that the Zen master can choose to offer to the individual already grappling with fundamental questions, but a classic one is the koan *mu*. This koan is known to have triggered the experience of awakening in countless individuals throughout history. Here I will offer some comments on this koan, following the tradition of my own continuing source spiritual nourishment, the Sanbo Kyodan Zen community—and keeping in mind that some readers are already familiar with Buddhist terminology and concepts, while others may have no familiarity with this tradition.

The text of the koan goes as follows: A monk asked Chao-chou (Joshu) in all earnestness, "Does a dog have Buddha nature?" To which Chao-chou replied: *"Mu."*[2]

It must be pointed out that, according to a basic Mahayana Buddhist tenet, all living beings are endowed with Buddha nature, or the capacity for enlightenment. Since a dog is a living being, we might expect Chao-chou to say: "Yes, indeed, a dog does have Buddha nature." But Chao-chou's answer, in the original Chinese, appears to be a negation: "No, not at all!" "No way!"

So, right there, the practitioner's mind is tantalized. Why does the Zen Master contradict Buddhist teaching? What is this *mu?* We are no longer talking about doctrinal matters. We are being told: "Your mission, should you decide to accept it, is to dissolve completely and become one with *mu*. From that vantage point, the answer to the question What is *mu?* will be clear. This answer must come out of your practice and not be theoretical or conceptual. And when it comes, it will open your mind's eye and reveal your true self." This is quite an intriguing invitation, indeed!

In those intensive Zen retreats, or sesshin, that last from five to eight days, practical preliminaries are given on the opening night, after which the Zen teacher would normally give a talk (called a *teisho*) on the koan *mu* to help practitioners deal with this practice.[3] A talk given in a Zen retreat would not be about theoretical or philosophical issues that would only lead practitioners away from the task at hand. It would be given in the spirit of the third mark, or cardinal principle, of Zen: that is, "pointing directly to the core of the human mind." A *teisho* always addresses issues of life and death and serves as a "pointer" to awaken the practitioner to one's true, integral self.

The Zen master may repeat the advice of Wu-men:

> *So, then, make your whole body a mass of doubt, and with your three hundred and sixty bones and joints and your eighty-four thousand hair follicles, concentrate on this one word mu. Day and night, keep digging into it. Don't consider it to be "nothingness." Don't think in terms of "has" and "has not." It is like swallowing a red-hot iron ball. You try to vomit it out, but you can't.*[4]

Indispensable to this practice is the one-on-one guidance of a Zen master who has been through this painstaking process and continued Zen practice for many years. (In this context, a person with ten to twenty years of experience would still be considered a beginner!) The Zen master can therefore point out the highroads, inroads, and pitfalls of this journey into the discovery of the true self. This one-on-one guidance is given in formal interview sessions (called *dokusan*).

Meanwhile, in sitting practice (zazen), we are enjoined to put our whole being, indefatigably and with every breath, into *mu*— even without the least idea what it could be. We are, perhaps, better off not having any idea what this could be, since the point is to not deal with ideas, thoughts, or images. The point is to dispose ourselves to direct experience, an experience that opens our eyes to the reality of who or what we are.

During meditation, we are instructed to inhale deeply but normally and exhale slowly, while uttering quietly within oneself, *"Muuuuuuu."* In this way every breath is guided by *mu,* and *mu* serves as the knot that ties one's whole being together, enabling everything else to fall into place. There is no image to attach to this *mu*—except, perhaps, as a distraction for those who cannot help but connect it with the image of a cow making its natural sound.

In this practice, we are not meant to obtain some thought, idea, or image about reality, no matter how lofty or profound. The point is the direct experience, the pure and simple *fact*, of being in the here and now. Realizing *this* with every breath, every step, every sensation, the opposition between subject and object is dissolved. This is very different than "understanding something" with our ordinary consciousness and its intellectual, subject-object mode of apprehension.

Between sitting periods, there are periods of the walking meditation (the Japanese word for which is *kinhin*). A practitioner of *mu* is advised to take every step while continuing to focus on *mu*. And in the context of retreat, we hold on to *mu* at every moment and in everything we do: getting up in the morning, going to the washroom, doing our chores, taking meals, taking a rest. We are encouraged to take Wu-men's advice literally: "Day and night, keep digging into it."

The intense nature of a Zen retreat offers many advantages. We have the privilege of practicing with a group of individuals who share the same motivation. Distractions that might serve as obstacles to singleminded practice—business, family, and other concerns—are set aside. And one or more interviews a day with the teacher can help clear away any obstacles to the absorption or dissolution into *mu*.

This is an atmosphere conducive to concentration. Here, we can gather ourselves together and literally melt into practice, into *mu*. This can be the occasion for an experiential breakthrough that opens us up to an entirely new world, "a new heaven and a new earth." (Rev. 21:1).

Outside of this context, we can set aside a period in during the day to sit in zazen posture, focus on the breath, and still the mind. Usually twenty-five minutes is a prescribed time frame, with a five-minute walk done in a meditative manner around the room or garden. We would continue with the utterance of *mu* with every exhalation of the breath, so that *mu* becomes part and parcel of our awareness of each breath, each step, each movement, and so on.

In this way, the distance between the practitioner and *mu* gradually closes, until it is no longer there. With the ripening of practice, *mu* no longer stands out as something extraneous to oneself; it melts into one's being as one breathes or moves about. With this dissolution into *mu*, the Zen Master's question answers itself: What is *mu?* The answer discovered by each practitioner is unique to each one. This is the discovery of one's own true self.

The Dynamics of Self-Discovery

One of the introductory talks given to beginners at San-un Zendo is about the parable of Enyadatta. It offers practitioners insight into the dynamics of the discovery of *mu.*

In this parable, a beautiful young maiden spends hours a day before the mirror, admiring her own beauty. But one day when she looks into the mirror, she is unable to see the reflection of her head. This causes her deep anxiety. Frantically she searches for her head. "Where is my head? What happened to my head?" she asks her friends. They, of course, reassure her: "Why, it is right there where it should be."

This bolsters her self-confidence somewhat, but she still can't see it for herself. So one day a friend gives her a blow to the head and, in pain and surprise, Enyadatta utters "Ouch!" With this, her friends point out that her head is right there. And Enyadatta awakens to the fact that it was there all along—and is greatly exhilarated and joyful.[5]

This parable illustrates what happens when we awaken to our true self in the practice of *mu*. What we find has been there right from the start but, for whatever reason, it's been hidden from view. The friends in the parable are like the Zen teachers or fellow practitioners who reassure us that it's there. This bolsters our confidence, even if we've not yet realized it for ourselves. Our actual discovery of the true self, however, liberates us from all delusions. Now we can live with our head held high. This realization is joyful and exhilarating; we may break out in laughter at our own stupidity for not having seen what's been here all along. Or we may give in to tears of joy, that we have now truly come home.

In one sense, there is nothing new here; it has been here from the beginningless beginning. In another sense, everything is new. We are seeing things from an entirely new perspective, and not from the standpoint of an I-consciousness in opposition to everything else in the universe. In the experience of true self-realization, the subject-object dichotomy is overcome. We grasp clearly the point of the Buddhist Wisdom sutras, like the famous Heart Sutra, that says: there is "no eye, ear, nose, tongue, body, mind; no color, sound, smell, taste, touch, thing."[6]

Here, a philosophically inclined reader might prefer a further theoretical explanation of this perspective that deals with going beyond the subject-object dichotomy. Numerous works on Buddhist philosophy seek to offer this. Most of these works center on a key term used to describe this domain and implications: *shunyata,* or "emptiness."[7] But let us desist from further speculating about this. It is helpful to be reminded that the structure of the Zen enlightenment experience presents, not the attainment of a state that was never there before, but the simple recovery—or perhaps better, the un-covering—of something that had been there all along.

Regarding the way we humans come to truth or the truth comes to us, philosopher Martin Heidegger similarly referred to the Greek term, *aletheia* (German, *Ent-deckung*), or "uncovering."[8] And those familiar with T. S. Eliot's *"Four Quartets"* will recall these lines:

> We shall not cease from our explorations
> And the end of all our exploring
> Will be to arrive where we started
> And know the place for the first time.[9]

Hearing the Way

The experience of awakening at the heart of Zen is not an attainment, properly speaking. We could describe it as an *event* that happens, when the conditions leading up to it ripen. Rather than an end-product or result of assiduous seeking or practice, it's a simple "letting be": a being-with and seeing through "what is," as the obstacles preventing this are removed.

The indefatigable effort called for in practice is not so much to bring about the enlightenment experience (as a result), but rather, simply to do our part in removing these obstacles. The greatest block to seeing "what is" is the separative I-consciousness that we imagine to be "in here," confronting the objects in a world "out there." Little by little, Zen practice whittles away this I-consciousness, showing it to be totally empty of any real content. Once the I-consciousness is seen through, each and every thing can be manifest "just as it is."

In one of his Zen talks, Yamada Roshi told a true story of a Japanese lady in her sixties, who had been stricken with an ailment that led to prolonged hospitalization. One night, after several weeks in her hospital bed, she was struggling with great physical pain and unable to fall asleep. All through the night, there was nothing that she could do but lie there with her eyes open, gazing at the wall as the sound of the clock went *tick tock, tick tock, tick tock.*

Then all of a sudden and without knowing why, toward the wee hours of morning, with the continuing sound of *tick tock, tick tock . . .*, she was overcome by a deep feeling of peace and exhilaration, accompanied by tears of joy and gratitude and a sense of acceptance of herself and her pain.

Relatives and friends who visited her in the following days noticed the great difference in her attitude and bearing. She was at peace with herself and was more open and sensitive toward others. When they remarked on this, she told them of her sudden experience, triggered by *tick tock, tick tock.* This was the turning point in her changed way of being.

Hearing this, a friend who was practicing Zen under a teacher close to Yamada Roshi suggested she visit this teacher to have her experience checked in the usual Zen procedure. And upon leaving the hospital, she did this, although she had not been a regular practitioner before. Sure enough, upon the usual questioning of Zen experiences, the Zen master confirmed that hers was a genuine experience of realization.

It is significant to note that this lady was not at all formally asking questions like "Who am I?" or "What is my true self?" Nor did she bring such questioning to any intentional meditative practice. She did not seem to be explicitly seeking answers to these questions. Of course, given her prolonged illness and the suffering it brought, we can only surmise that she had her own struggles with basic issues of life and death, the meaning of her life, and the question of human suffering.

Living with physical pain and having to lie in a hospital bed in patience and long-suffering became, for her, way of undergoing a process of inner purification. Thus her ego had mellowed and had become more and more transparent. The *tick tock, tick tock* during that crucial night simply triggered her discovery of her true self, of the realm of interconnectedness, wherein the whole universe is clear and transparent in this moment, and there is no separation of the hearer and the heard.

The experience of enlightenment in Zen cuts through the dichotomy that our ordinary conscious mind creates between the hearer and the heard, seer and seen, subject and object.

A koan targeting the separation of the hearer and heard is called *Kikunushi,* or "The One that Hears," or more simply, "Who hears!" (These two words could be concluded by a question mark, an exclamation point, or a period, showing various angles in practice.) This koan simply invites us to *listen* with our whole being, to actually manifest "Who hears." We just sit in zazen and listen, with no sense of listening to something "out there" or "in here." With no distinction between the listening subject and heard object, simply listen and awaken to the "one who hears"—that is, the (no-) "one who hears."

With our whole being focused on "Who hears!"—and without a speck of distracting thoughts or mental images—we can see "without a speck of cloud to mar the gazing eye." We are disposed, in the here and now, for the momentous event of hearing the timeless word—the word, there in the beginning and there beyond the end of time (see John 1:1–18, Eph. 1:3–10). Hearing the primal word addressed to our being from the beginningless beginning is a transforming event that heals our state of alienation, and brings us home.

In Christian terms, by the light of grace, we are given a glimpse of the universe from the eyes of God. This glimpse enables us to bridge our supposed separation from God and thus heal our cosmic woundedness. With the gift of being able to truly hear, even for one instant, we manifest fully the "one who hears" as inseparable from the Word that is heard.

This reminds me of a famous Chinese saying that Japanese students learn in their junior high school textbooks: "Hearing the Way in the morning, one is ready to die at dusk." This bit of wisdom points out that hearing the way (Tao) is what life is all about; it marks the fulfillment of our life. Having thus known life in its fullness, hearing the way even once enables us to meet death with equanimity.

It is simply a matter of bracing ourselves: putting our whole being in the here and now, we allow our whole self to truly listen so the Way can be heard—and manifest, right here in the wounded, problem-filled, violence-prone world of our everyday life.

Just Sitting: Shikan Taza

The case of the Japanese lady described above is a helpful reminder that people arrive at the experience of enlightenment, or self-realization, from different frames of mind or intentionality. My own experience in guiding many Zen practitioners through the years has made me more fully aware of this fact. For the many consciously wrestling with basic questions of identity, these life and death questions are characteristic of their practice.

Others, however, are simply trying to find order in their lives, find their bearings, and be centered in whatever they do. For them, zazen is a powerful practice, leading one to find one's ground and become centered at the core of one's being. This practice becomes a habit of mind and naturally flows into all that we do. And while the fundamental questions ("Who am I?" "What is this all about?") may not be in the foreground of one's consciousness, these are nevertheless underlying presuppositions of the practice.

Instead of offering these practitioners koan practice, with its active pursuit of questions guided by the koan, a more effective practice would be *shikan taza,* or "just sitting," "simply sitting through and through," or "single-minded sitting."

This sitting practice may appear to be easy enough, but it is actually the most refined and difficult form of meditative practice. It is, in fact, the kind of sitting normally done by those who have already had an initial experience of awakening, who have glimpsed the world of enlightenment and deepened their realization in day-to-day life. "Just sitting" is a powerful form of practice that is an end in itself. It is an embodied manifestation of the world of enlightenment.

The Zen master Dogen speaks of the oneness of practice and enlightenment and points out their inseparability. Consider the following question-and-answer passage in his masterwork, the *Shobogenzo:*

> Question: *"Zazen may be an effective way of practice for those who have not yet realized enlightenment. But what about those who are already enlightened?"*
> Answer: *"It is said that we should not relate our dreams in front of fools or give oars to woodcutters, but I will try to answer your question. It is the view of the non-believers that practice and enlightenment are not one. But practice is itself enlightenment, and even the initial resolve to seek the Way already contains complete and perfect enlightenment. There is no enlightenment apart from practice. It is very important to realize this. Since practice is enlightenment, enlightenment is without end and practice is without beginning."*[10]

Here, Dogen makes the important point that Zen, which for him finds its quintessence in the practice of just sitting, is not a means to an end. Therefore the practice of zazen, or seated meditation, does not have the "goal" of attaining enlightenment; it is, itself, the very embodiment of enlightenment, the being and see-ing of things just as they are.

In philosophical terms, we can say that doing and being are no longer distinct; they are in complete and perfect oneness. One sits, just sits, breathing in and breathing out, with no purpose or goal. And in one's very sitting, one embodies the simple fact of pure be-ing. One's existence, in its totality, flows from pure be-ing—and right then and there, comes to self-realization.

In that very pure fact of "just sitting," we manifest the true self—flowing, like everything else, from pure be-ing. But this is not limited to just sitting. Having realized the true self in "just sit-ting," this continues as we stand up, as we do walking meditation, and as we proceed from meditation to the different activities of our life. In each moment of our twenty-four-hour day, we mani-fest the true self—as we get up in the morning, wash our face, take breakfast, drive to work, and so on.

Thus Zen practice overcomes separatedness and awakens us to a world of interconnectedness: a world where everything is real-ized as such, and where my "self" is inseparable from everything that is. This world of enlightenment—"just as it is," with every breath, every step, every smile and every tear—is replete with wonder and mystery at every moment.

All this sounds so simple. And we are invited to simply come and taste it for ourselves. Hard as it may be to believe, Zen prac-tice is an invitation, addressed to anyone and everyone, to a feast. This feast is a celebration of Being. And we're being invited to join the dance of the universe—in every moment of our lives, in everything we are and do.

What prevents us from being fully present for this celebration? It is only our delusive I-consciousness, the one-sided mistaken notion of self that separates us from everything else. Now we are invited to let go of this ego by unmasking it for what it is—a nonentity—and emptying ourselves of its sway over us.

This letting go of ego is the Zen experience of awakening. It liberates us from our attachment to the delusive I-consciousness—because there is nothing to be attached to. It is empty. Conversely, in seeing the I-consciousness as empty, we see everything in the universe in full relief. Without the filter of the I-consciousness, we see things *just as they are.* Seeing the interconnectedness of each and every thing, we see that everything is inseparable from "me." This heralds the actual experience of the true self.

Cosmic Affirmation: God Is Love

Here is an account of another facet of the experience of awakening. This extended quote is from a young German woman, born and raised in the Catholic tradition. She had come to do graduate research in Japan, where she practiced Zen at a temple in Kyoto and later under Yamada Roshi in Kamakura.

I had started doing Zen in Germany with Father Lassalle, a Jesuit priest. He gave me this koan mu, *and hinted to me that the answer to this koan points to oneself, to the answer to the question, "What is your self?"*

In Kyoto I went to practice Zen in a temple, and would go to this old master for interviews three times a week during evenings, and I would bring to him my answer to the koan. At every interview he would simply shake his head, and often he didn't even say a word, and so I would go out and feel very depressed, and sometimes even angry. This went on for about a year.

Then Father Lassalle had a sesshin *[intensive meditation retreat] in Tokyo, and I joined that one, in the summer of 1987. During this time, as I was sitting there, practicing with my koan* mu, *some voice told me,* God is Love.

Somehow for me there was this big question, if God is love, then how come I don't experience this? So I was fighting this voice. It was like fighting the koan mu, *because I knew, I didn't experience* mu *either. So I was sitting there, fighting* "God is Love, mu," "God is Love, mu," *and then suddenly I felt a terrible sense of being sorry, a sense of repentance. There I was, the most stupid being that had ever been on earth, for ever doubting that GOD IS LOVE.*

And then the answer was there completely! I mean, it was not a word or anything like that. Maybe you can describe it like being touched by God. And it is a really real thing to experience it. So I jumped up and I knew the answer to my koan, and rushed to the interview room and I said, "this is it."

And he (Fr. Lassalle) said to me, "How did you know?" And he confirmed that it was the right answer.

But the interesting thing is that when you find the answer for yourself, you experience it as if everybody else did experience the same thing, because you know it is the same reality for everyone else. And yet everyone else is just as stupid as you in not knowing. From this sense that you feel so stupid yourself, there comes that deep sense of compassion with all the other stupid beings who are so full of grace and full of God's love and yet just like you yourself are fighting against it. This is the way I would describe my experience, confirmed later by Yamada Roshi.

It is worth noting here that this woman's experience is triggered by a phrase so familiar to Christians. Yet for so many it rings hollow. The words *God is love* evoke many different things, from a sense of assurance and comfort for some, to a sense of doubt and even positive rejection in others: "If God is love, how can there be so much suffering, evil, and hate in the world? How can God allow such situations of misery and the continuing destruction of his own creation?"

It is only when these words cease to be mere words—as when the sound of *mu* ceases to be "meaningless" and becomes our whole being—that it dawns on us: "This is it!"

Zen awakening is the experience of "This is it!" in our lives. It's not the words, but the true "This is it!" experience that can't be expressed in words. (I caution astute practitioners who may read this and simply repeat these words as an attempted answer in their Zen interview: No, the mere words will not do.) The power of this experience can overturn our whole being. It can pull the rug out from under our delusive ego that keeps fighting the reality of who we truly are, the reality that *God is Love.*

Paul Tillich's remarkable essay titled "You Are Accepted" resonates with this kind of experience. Tillich writes that our human situation of sin is a state of separation from the Ground of Being and from one another.[11] Nothing we can *do* can bridge the chasm separating us from our ground. Our attempts or efforts only widen the gap. This is because they issue from our egoistic desire to "do good" so that we can "feel good" and justify self-complacency. Instead if we admit to our state of separation and our powerlessness in it, we open ourselves to the pure touch of grace: a voice from the depths of our being whispers, "You are accepted."

And so we are called to do *nothing* but simply accept the fact that we are accepted! The Good News can come home to us and transform our lives. "This is it!" And we know, in every pore of our being, that *God is Love* is not a hair's breadth apart from the reality that we are.

"You are accepted." This message of cosmic affirmation has constantly been addressing us from all eternity. When our proud egos stop resisting and simply accept this fact—we are accepted just as we are—a new dawn breaks in our lives.

This is the dawning of *God is Love* in our lives. We are accepted by the very love that makes the universe what it is. This is our joyous discovery of the treasure in the field, described in the Gospel of Matthew:

> *The reign of heaven is like treasure hidden in a field,*
> *which someone found and covered up. Then in one's joy one*
> *goes and sells all one has, and buys that field (Mt 13:44).*

To sell all we have is to empty ourselves of everything that stands in the way, beginning with our ego. Having "sold everything" pertaining to this ego, we are enabled to make that field and its treasure our own.

With no delusive egoic self separating us from the rest of the world, we finally come "home". We are at home with ourselves, and we're at home in the universe, right where we are. This at-home-ness is accompanied by a deep, deep peace—a peace that can never be taken away.

5

Embodying the Way

ZEN SPIRITUALITY blossoms in the actualization of the awakening experience in our day-to-day life. This is called "embodying the peerless way." The following koan captures what is involved in such a way of life.

> *A monk said to Chao-chou, "I have just entered this*
> *monastery. Please instruct me."*
> *Chao-chou said, "Have you had your breakfast?"*
> *The monk replied, "Yes, I have."*
> *Chao-chou said, "Wash your bowls."*
> *The monk realized .*[1]

This koan elucidates key aspects of the Zen way of life and the way it relates to our healing. It begins with the earnest request of the novice monk who has just entered the monastery: "Please instruct me." If we put ourselves in the shoes of this monk, we can see what the koan is about.

First, we must note that entering the monastery is a major decision to set aside worldly pursuits of wealth, power, and fame, and give ourselves wholeheartedly to the One Thing Necessary. The subject of this koan has taken this step to open himself/herself to the realization of what really matters in life. Nothing less than such a great resolve—and a readiness to be totally transformed and to live life in accord with the demands of one's true self—will be adequate.

Koan study places us in a continuous line of persons who have given themselves wholeheartedly to the pursuit of liberating truth. Cutting through time and culture, we are called to assume no less a state of mind. And some of us actually do enter a monastery, either for a limited period or for life.

Almost all of the koans in the main Zen traditions are from episodes and anecdotes of the lives of monks. (Sadly, few of these characters from received sources are women.)[2] Many Zen monasteries now have active communities of practicing monks, male and female, in Asia, America, and Europe. In China, the original context of this koan, entrance into a monastery was the socially supported way available for the single-minded pursuit of truth for many individuals. Until the proscription of organized religion in China by the Communist authorities, Buddhist monasteries flourished, as did a few Christian monastic communities. The Tibetan Buddhist tradition is still kept alive in its monasteries by devout and learned monks both in and out of Tibet. A similar mode of life can be found in ashrams in India, where one can live a simple life in a supportive community bound by common pursuits.

In the Christian tradition, monastic life has always been an esteemed path. Although their numbers have been dwindling in the past two or three decades, monastic life continues to be a valuable fount of spiritual resources for the worldwide Christian community.[3]

In recent years, monastic men and women from different religious traditions have been exchanging invitations to reside for short periods of time in their monasteries, to engage in interreligious monastic dialogue. Zen monks from Japan have lived briefly in European Christian monasteries and invited Christian monks to their Zen temples in Japan. Similar ventures are also being undertaken in the United States, under the auspices of the Monastic Inter-religious Dialogue (MID) network. These mutual exchanges include Christian monastics from Benedictine and Trappist orders among others, and Tibetan Buddhist and Zen monks, as well as Hindu monastics.[4]

There are various experiments in modified forms of monastic living involving not only male and female celibates, but married couples with their families as well. These undertakings are attempts to forge a way of life in community that are supportive of the common pursuit of truth, social justice, and a simple and ecologically sound way of life.[5]

When the koan calls us to put ourselves in the place of the person just entering a monastery, we are invited to plunge ourselves wholeheartedly to the pursuit of truth, and in so doing, to realize the fullness of life.

As a koan practitioner, we need not be literally one of those privileged ones able to follow the monastic path. However, koan practice does demand an unrelenting dedication to pursuing our truth, as a matter of ultimate concern. Even if we're not called to monastic life in the formal sense, we are called to awaken to truth, to awaken the mystery of our existence here on Earth. Zen is concerned with nothing less than this.

Genuine Zen practice is not some kind of hobby or spare-time activity for enhancing physical or mental health or relieving stress, like aerobics or yoga. This is not to look down upon those who come to Zen with this initial motivation. But as our practice deepens, Zen challenges our entire being, and confronts us with the matter of life and death itself. The monk's earnest request is about a matter of life and death: "Please teach me." That is, "Please teach me not only the rubrics of the monastic way of life, but all about the basic mystery of life, about the resolution of this matter of life and death. This is why I am here."

Zen Master Chao-chou's response is curt and to the point. "Have you had your breakfast?" I should note that the question "Have you had your meal?" is also a form of greeting in China. But Chao-chou is not making a casual greeting or exchanging pleasantries. Zen koans are always about life and death matters. Of course you might ask skeptically, "How could a trivial question about one's breakfast be a matter of life and death?" This is the first checkpoint of the koan. Our mode of awareness is being challenged here.

Chao-chou's question hits right to the heart of the matter itself, the basic mystery of life. In veiled Zen talk it is asking "Have you met your true self?" or "Have you become awakened?" "Are you now satisfied?" "Have you had your fill?" And if you've not yet "had your breakfast," the implication is that, without further ado, you should. For this, Zen practice provides us with a clear and systematic "recipe." The three main ingredients are a posture conducive to stillness; awareness of our breathing; and quieting the mind by focusing on the here and now. Setting up our daily life to be conducive to practice completes the preparation.

Each of us has a unique way of preparing this "meal." We may take weeks, months, or years to put the ingredients together so we really get a taste of our breakfast. And it makes a crucial difference to have the guidance of an experienced cook. A teacher with whom we consult regularly can effect change in our entire life. This is what true Zen teachers are for. (Again, I bow repeatedly in gratitude to my own teacher, the late Koun Yamada Roshi, who gave of himself totally and unreservedly to those who sought his guidance in Zen practice.)

Here I will remind the reader that chapter three of this book deals with the essentials of Zen practice. The previous chapter describes the pivotal enlightenment experience and an approach to "taking our breakfast"—Zen-style.

Interestingly, "getting our fill" in Zen means *emptying* ourselves: as in emptying a bowl filled with a lifetime of delusive thinking and inauthentic living.[6] This is what the practice of sitting meditation is about. Guided by the breath, it brings us to a life lived in tune with the present moment. "Have you had your breakfast?" "Yes, I have," the monk answers. He had done his homework, and had reaped its fruit.

At first reading, a koan may give us the impression this is all a piece of cake—or bowl of oatmeal. But, like preparing a meal, much preparation went into the monk's answer. Then we must cook and actually enjoy our meal before can we say, "Yes, now I'm satisfied."

Another example of the tremendous amount of practice behind these curt responses is the koan entitled "Bodhidharma and Peace of Mind." Here the founder of Zen (Bodhidharma) is earnestly sought by Hui-k'o, the man destined to become the Second Ancestor of Zen in China. Hui-k'o was already approaching middle age at the time of this encounter:

> *"Please, sir, your disciple's mind is not yet at peace. I beg you, my teacher, please give it peace."*
> *Bodhidharma replied, "Bring that mind to me, and I will give it peace."*
> *"I have searched for the mind, and I cannot find it."*
> *"There, I have completely set it at rest for you."*[7]

As do most koans, this one deals with a matter of ultimate concern. A surface reading may give the impression that this is just one exchange. But when Second Ancestor confesses that he has searched for mind and cannot find it, it is clear that much tedious leg-folding, breathing, and quieting the mind paved the way for this answer. Bodhidharma's concluding response affirms Second Ancestor's realization of true peace of mind—and the indefatigable practice that preceded it.

But what in heaven's name is going on here, you may ask. Didn't the disciple just say "I cannot find it"? How can Bodhidharma pat him and say "There, I have completely set it at rest for you"? This is no mere word-play, but an invitation to experience the gap—the gap between the disciple's "I cannot find it" and Bodhidharma's "There, I have completely set it at rest for you." This gap is precisely what we must experience for ourselves. This "gap" may consist of weeks, months, or even years of assiduous sitting practice, asking, "Who am I?" "Where is this mind that is not at peace?" "What is this anyway?"

By practicing wholeheartedly, as a matter of life and death, we come to that very point where *"I cannot find it"* and "There, I have completely set it at rest for you" converge. With nothing—no space, idea, or concept—separating the thrust and the parry, or to take another Zen image, as the two arrows meet in mid-air, one arrives at the pure "zero-point." Here, that which has always been there simply comes to the fore.

As we've seen above, this can be triggered by anything under the sun. But no matter how it comes to us—or we come to it—it is Earth-shaking: accompanied by exhilaration, emotional outbursts, laughter, tears, even convulsions; or experienced simply as deep inner peace, and the sheer liberating joy of having come to our own.

This is the actual fullness of having "had our meal"—such that we will never again go hungry. This is the deep inner peace that no one can take away. Likewise, it is the experience of the "living water" Jesus promised to the woman of Samaria when he met her by the well and said: "Drinking of this water of eternal life, one will no longer thirst" (John 4:14).

Having persevered in the struggle with aching legs, stray thoughts, and the myriad other things that come up in sitting practice, we've had an exquisite taste of what Zen actually offers. And we have felt the wholesome effects of sitting practice in our daily life. This brings us to a stage of enhanced fervor. Naturally, we want to tell everybody else to try this practice. But now we are invited to engage in the lifelong task of deepening of our practice further, ever cultivating what is called "beginner's mind."[8]

It is quite easy to become attached to the effects of the transformative experience. Instead of moving on to the next step, we might want to keep coming back to it; pin it on our lapel, so to speak; count it among our possessions; or turn it into cocktail party conversation. To this, Chao-chou says: "Wash your bowls!"

Yamada Roshi repeatedly cautioned those whose enlightenment experience he himself had confirmed: this experience is comparable to entering the first-grade in elementary school. It is the first step on a lifelong or, better, *infinitely* long path leading deeper and deeper into the mystery of life and death. Of course, it is easy for first-graders to feel proud of being there. But that pride would be misplaced. Misplaced pride—coupled with an inordinate zeal to talk about Zen, even to the disinterested and out of proper context—is aptly termed "Zen sickness." Whether relatively mild or mortally grave, it is easy to spot.

So, feeling fulfilled after our breakfast of nice soft oatmeal, we now must wash our bowls. Otherwise the remnants dry up and produce a stink. This image of old, dried oatmeal is frequently repeated by Susan Jion Postal, a Zen priest and teacher who leads a group in New Rochelle, New York. She cautions those who come to Zen looking for another spiritual trip, or a feather in their cap, or spiritual treasure to add to their collection alongside of yoga, macrobiotics, *feng shui,* or what have you—soon stink like weeks-old dried porridge.[9]

The late Chögyam Trungpa, a well-known Tibetan Buddhist master, also cautioned against what he called "spiritual material-ism": a subtle form of self-deception wrapped in good inten-tions.[10] Similarly, Saint John of the Cross talks of the "spiritual avarice" that bogs us down in the dark night of the soul.[11] Such problems all stem from an attachment to "spiritual goods." Attachment can even develop toward the spiritual teacher who helps us on the path, thus hampering our spiritual liberation.[12]

It is crucial to purify attachment through continued sitting prac-tice—especially after our initial taste of the "zero-point." This enables us to ripen into the wholesome, simple life of true Zen. After the initial experience of awakening, continuing koan practice addresses the sheen that may accompany that experience and brings us back to the ordinary life of a normal human being. Like anyone else, we go about our life, getting up in the morning, going to work, getting tired, relaxing, laughing, and crying. The difference, now, is that we are no longer deluded by false ideas of the self.

A life lived in its ordinariness can be replete with a sense of wonder and mystery at every turn. Having, in the light of zero-point, seen through the empty nature of the self, we can now see the connectedness of the true self with everything else, and the connectedness of everything in this universe with that self—or, more properly speaking, no-self.

From the realization of interconnectedness naturally flowers a life of compassion: a *suffering-with* all beings in the universe, who are no longer seen as separate from us.

To keep our eyes open to the miracle of the ordinary, right before us every moment of our lives, we must "wash our bowls"—day by day, moment to moment. This is a process of not clinging to any-thing at all, not even our spiritual possessions. By continuing to let go, we can be open to the newness of every moment, with every breath we are given. In Zen, washing one's bowls means living every moment in its freshness, and in celebration of its mystery.

To Become As Little Children

Someone in Japan once told me about a young father and his little three-year-old daughter, taking a Sunday stroll one day in Spring. Walking hand in hand through a meadow, they came upon a clearing with clusters of violets. The little girl broke loose from her father's hand and began to prance about among the flowers. "Look, Daddy, look!"

The father, watching with quiet pride and a knowing air, said: "Yes, dear, those are violets." The little girl continued dancing and prancing, uttering the new word "Violets! Violets!"

The point here is the difference between their modes of awareness. The little girl, wide-eyed and full of wonder, saw the flowers in their pristine beauty before she could name them. The beauty right before her simply moved her to dance. The joy and celebration of being-with was unsullied by dualistic thoughts or frame of mind. This awareness of the simple beauty of nature is filled with mystery and wonder.

Her father, on the other hand, now wise in the ways of the world, "knew" that those flowers were violets—and in so knowing, thereby lost the ability to see their freshness and mystery. "Those are violets": the human capacity to name things takes its toll on our mode of awareness. While gaining a certain sense of control over the things we can name, we lose the sense of their mystery and wonder.

"Why are there existing things rather than nothing?" Martin Heidegger asks in the very first line of his book *Introduction to Metaphysics*.[13] Rather than demanding an answer, such a question evokes a quality of awareness that throws light on our very mode of being.

To fail to raise such a question—or to bury it in mundane pre-occupations such as getting ahead, making a profit, making a name for ourselves, and so on—is to become less than what we really are as human beings. Getting lost in the business of securing our livelihood, we lose our life. The malady of Western civilization, ventured Heidegger, is the "forgetfulness of Being."

The question "Why are there things rather than nothing?" is a way of expressing our awareness of the mystery that we are, the mystery that is this universe. And it will not be quenched by responding "Because such and such is the case, therefore. . . ." Nor is it solved by traditional religious formulas, such as "God made all things out of nothing." Any child will immediately counter, "Then who made God?" Such traditional formulas are like the father's response to his little daughter dancing with the violets: they replace a sense of mystery with ready-made explanations.

Unfortunately, we have already lost our innocence. The process of "education" by which we learn how to live in this world teaches us to name things, and it leads us to think we can in this way master everything in the universe. The "higher" our education, the farther we are taken from a sense of wonder and mystery.

With our self-understanding now based on the separation and distinctions of naming, we feel acutely isolated and alienated from the universe. "I" am here; all others—including all human beings—are objects confronting me, outside of me.

This frame of mind leads to a desire for control, due to the deep anxiety brought on by a sense of separateness. Out of alienation and insecurity also comes a deep longing to reconnect. But trying to overcome separateness through power and control over the world, its inhabitants, and nature as a whole is an entirely misguided attempt. It only manages to deepen the gulf and deepen the woundedness at the core of our being.

The very desire for knowledge, in the sense of knowing this universe, comes from a deep longing to reconnect. Not knowing causes us to feel insecure, even threatened. So we pursue what Aristotle called the natural human desire to know. In this spirit, at the beginning of the so-called Modern Age of human history, Francis Bacon proclaimed that "knowledge is power." This dubious power, coming out of objective knowledge, has led our Earth community to where we are today: the brink of destruction.

By exercising what we understood to be our God-given prerogative to name the things of this universe, we lost their sense of mystery and *God-givenness*. Advancement in knowledge, with its corollary increase in our power over nature, has led us to de-sacralize everything in the universe. With a sense of wonder, a sense of sacredness was lost—including the sacredness of "violets."

Is there is no escaping our seeming prerogative and distinctive human trait of naming the things around us? Is there no way back to the pristine state of original innocence and wonder? Having "eaten of the fruit of the tree of knowledge of good and evil," can we seek salvation in a simple return to a pristine state before such "knowing"? And, if not, what salvation is there for us?

When the little girl learns to name those beautiful flowers, she exclaims "Violets! Violets!"—and continues dancing. Naming them did not necessarily take away her awareness of the mystery, wonder, and beauty of the flowers. The dance, in fact, acquired a new quality with her ability to properly address those with whom she was dancing, "Violets! Violets!"

Thus this dancing little girl shows us that perhaps there is a way to recover our sense of mystery. Perhaps those of us who have lost our innocence, known separation, and learned the ways of the world *can* learn to dance again with the violets. Morris Berman called this, in a book that made ripples when it came out some years ago, the "the re-enchantment of the world."[14]

Learning the names of flowers does not mean we have any power over them at all. "Even Solomon, in all his glory, was not arrayed like one of these" (Mt 6:29), we are reminded by the Bible. For all our self-serving ways to alter the genes of plants, animals, and even human beings, it is not now nor will it ever be within our power to call them into being.

What is, unfortunately, within our power is to cause them to *cease* to be. Thousands of species are ceasing to be as a result of our way of living and relating to the Earth. We cannot but shudder at our "power"—all rooted in separateness and our misguided attempts to overcome it. This deep-seated longing to reconnect with our world needs to be redirected to its original course. We need, in other words, to learn to once again dance with the violets.

"Unless you become as these little children, you shall not enter the reign of God" (Mt 18:3). Jesus' words invite us to recover a mode of being, a mode of awareness that will heal our cosmic woundedness.

The Wonder of a Cup of Tea

In a spurious but revelatory story of a fictional International Meditators' Convention, adept meditators from various traditions were invited to present the best of what they had to offer. The finalists were narrowed down to three: the first two were from Eastern traditions which will remain unnamed here; the third was a Zen monk from Japan.

The first of the finalists took the stage, went into a trance, and within minutes could be seen levitating six inches above the floor, cushion and all! Within minutes, this adept settled back on the stage, came out of the trance, stood up, and bowed to a standing ovation.

The second finalist took the cushion and likewise, within minutes, went into deep meditation. Then an assistant let out a swarm of gigantic mosquitoes from a bottle. The mosquitoes swooped upon the second finalist and began biting from every angle. But the adept was not moved, remaining in meditation until the mosquitoes grew tired and found their way out of the arena. Again, a standing ovation as the second finalist awoke from the trance refreshed, without so much as a mosquito bite.

Then the third finalist, the Zen monk from Japan, was called in. Bowing first to the assistants on stage and then to the audience, he took a seat on the round cushion at the center of the stage. Assuming a cross-legged posture, breathing normally yet deeply, the monk sat quietly in Zen meditation. All eyes were focused on the meditator. And everyone was in silence as if partaking in his inner peace and silence. Then, after twenty-five minutes, an assistant rang a bell. The monk joined his palms in a gesture of reverence and made a bow to the audience. The assistant came in with a cup of tea on a tray. He offered it to the monk, who again bowed in gratitude, sipped the tea, and smiled at the audience saying, "Ah, delicious. Thank you very much."

Fully attentive, the audience waited for something spectacular to happen, as with the two previous contestants. But the Zen monk simply had another serving of tea and returned the cup. Again giving thanks, he bowed and left the stage. For a while, the audience remained in silence. Then, one by one, they began nodding in recognition and smiling and nodding to one another—enwrapped in a peaceful, reassuring sense of having rediscovered something very precious.

It took time for the audience to realize what had come over them: the deep sense of satisfaction at glimpsing the grand fruit of Zen life, which the monk embodied in his simple presence. Sitting quietly, taking one's tea, being grateful, exiting—that is all. No fireworks or spectacular displays; just opening our eyes to the miracle of it all, the wonder of a cup of tea.

This story was, of course, evidently one concocted by someone sympathetic to the Zen tradition. But the point is brought home nonetheless: Zen is not for those who expect spectacular results from meditation, such as the attainment of superhuman powers. Of course, these are not precluded, if they come naturally as the unsought fruit of long years of practice. But this is not what Zen is about. The best that Zen has to offer cannot be fathomed by those looking to Zen with an ulterior motive.

Even the experience of enlightenment, or *kensho,* is not a goal to be sought or attained through our own efforts. It is, of course, a totally transformative kind of experience, and it is what draws us to Zen. But if we regard it as some goodie, consumer item, or scout merit badge we want to pin on our lapel, we will become sidetracked and miss the whole point.

What Zen offers is an invitation to "taste and see." It offers the quiet joy of simply being. *Just that*—whether sitting, standing, walking, laughing, crying. It is getting up in the middle of the night to soothe a crying baby back to sleep; waking up in the morning and going to work. It is playing with the children and listening to music. It is putting out the garbage—sorting out plastics and bottles for recycling—and writing a letter to one's senator, joining a picket line, or lining up in a soup kitchen. It is getting tired, growing old, battling with cancer, dying of AIDS or of a heart attack. *Just that*—and in the midst of it, experiencing a miracle.

To embody the way of awakening in our daily life is nothing more than living every moment, just as it is, empty of ego and filled with a sense of mystery and wonder.

I am reminded of an incident in my mid-teens, when I was on my way to an open-air dance party in my hometown in the Philippines. I was walking side-by-side with a friend I'll call Al, who was in his first year of medical school at the time. My heart was already thumping with expectation as we neared the plaza where the dance was to be held. As we walked along, Al began telling me about an anatomy class he had the day before. They had dissected a human cadaver, opening the torso and examining the lungs, heart, liver, and other internal organs, as the instructor explained their functions. What Al wanted to share with me was how profoundly this had impressed him: this human body, structured in such a delicate and marvelous way that we humans have never been able to completely figure out. He could only look on in awe and wonder. The human body had brought him face-to-face with something infinitely mysterious, the truly "unthinkable" complex of our bodies.

Al's reaction touched a deep chord within me. I recall my heart thumping excitedly with a new awareness: the awareness of mystery of our being.

When we finally reached the plaza, we joined the dance and the party went on. But for me that night, the band played a different kind of music and the stars had a different kind of glow.[15]

It was not a matter of simply concluding "Therefore there is a God." Rather, based on the conceptual framework of my traditional Roman Catholic upbringing, the term "God" took on a new meaning. It was not a question of holding on to a notion or definition of "God." It was a sensing, deep within, that there is unfathomable Wisdom in all this; that there is a point to the existence of the universe; and that, ultimately, *we are in good hands.*

This sense of "unthinkable . . ." remained with me, becoming more clear and distinct as I was led further into Zen. In Zen practice, we become aware that every heartbeat, every breath, every hair on our head—as well as every newborn baby, blade of grass, and pebble on the road—is an "unthinkable" miracle.

It is the recovery of wonder and mystery that can heal our rift with nature, ourselves, and our fellow human beings. Living every moment in this mode of awareness brings a vivid sense of connectedness with the universe.

6

This Is My Body

ZEN PRACTICE—with its attention given to posture, breathing, and focus on the here and now—makes us more deeply sensitive to the miracle of this very body.

In this chapter, we will explore the dimensions of Zen practice in "this very body." In this way, we may better see its cosmic implications and glimpse its "breadth and length and height and depth" (Eph. 3:18). Thus we may not only recover a sense of the body's sacredness, we may also find the way to heal its brokenness.

Dropping Off Body and Mind

In the closing lines of the eighteenth-century Zen master Hakuin's "Song of Zazen," which is chanted all over the world, we find reference to "this very body":

*At this moment, what is it you seek? Nirvana is
right here before you. Lotus Land is right here.
This very body, the body of the Buddha.*[1]

The "Song of Zazen," which expresses the heart of Zen enlightenment in a beautiful and poetic way, conveys a powerful message: "Do not look outside of yourself, no need to look afar: what
you seek is right here, right where you are."[2]

Zen practice focuses our whole being, and all that involves, in
the here and now by following our breath. Now this is not as simple as it sounds. If we've practiced, even for a little while, we realize we are dispersed in so many directions, and the various
elements of our being are often at odds with one another. In other
words, we are not fully there.

The most basic opposition we encounter in ourselves is the one
between "body" and "mind." Our body may be sitting in meditation posture, but within a few minutes our mind may wander to
another dimension. A stray thought can take us off to a past experience, an anticipated event, or something happening (or not happening) right now.

Zazen invites us to experience body and mind, not in a separated and oppositional way, but as an organic, dynamic unity. As
we sit with our back straight and legs folded in a relaxed but
attentive posture, our mind is fully aware. And with each breath,
time ceases to be seen as a linear series of present moments reced-
ing into the past; it is experienced as an ever present *now*.

As our practice deepens, we can glimpse the world of body-
mind non-opposition; a world where, in the great Zen master
Dogen's words, the body and mind "drop off."

*To learn the way of the awakened is to learn the self.
To learn the self is to forget the self.
To forget the self is to perceive the self in all things.*

To perceive the self in all things is to drop off one's own body-mind
  as well as to drop off the other's body-mind.
As one reaches this, there is no more trace of enlightenment,
  but one simply lives
This enlightenment-without-a-trace.[3]

According to written accounts, "dropping off body-mind" is the expression that triggered Dogen's own enlightenment experience, recognized by his teacher, Ju-ching, in China. In his short account of the "way of the awakened," there are clues to this dimension that Dogen is inviting us to experience for ourselves.

First, the way of the awakened is none other than the realization of our true self. The true self cannot be conceived of as a substance or entity "out there" or "in here." It is not waiting to be discovered; it is realized precisely by forgetting it altogether. *Forgetting the self* breaks down the imagined wall we've placed between our self and everything else in the universe. This is the "dropping off" of our own body-mind.

Dropping off our own body-mind also means dropping off the body-mind of "other." What remains? Not a single trace of enlightenment as a self-conscious attitude or mental framework, but simply a raw actualization of every concrete event in our daily life.

"This very body, the body of the Buddha" in Hakuin's "Song of Zazen" does not invite speculation or intellectual leaps that equate "this very body" with some conceptual "body of the Buddha." These would lead to bloated or presumptuous statements like "my body is the Buddha-body"—and nothing could be further from true awakening than this.

Dogen's true awakening, or "dropping off body-mind," is actualized in *forgetting* of one's self. This is the paradox we are invited to enter: to forget one's self, and in that forgetting of self, to realize awakening. "This very body, the body of the Buddha," is in all the very mundane yet wondrous events of breathing, standing, sitting, walking, laughing, crying, and so on. In more technical language, this direct mode of awareness breaks through the subject-object barrier created by our separative I-consciousness, which assumes a self as subject "in here" looking at objects "out there"—including our own body. From this point of view, we "have" a body, which we control and move about at will. This "common-sense" understanding of a self vis-a-vis the world has prevailed in Western philosophical tradition, especially since Descartes.

Seeing the self in opposition to the body, the world, and to God has long been the dominant Western worldview. And it underlies our presumptuous attempts to conquer and control nature. Now, with an acute sense of our alienation from nature, our bodies, and our deepest selves, we are coming to realize the fallacy and self-destructive effects of this subject-object dichotomy. In recent decades, developments in Western phenomenology, philosophy, and theology have opened the way for the retrieval of an awareness of body: body as a lived body, a body that I "am" rather than "have."[4] (In Eastern traditions, being less prone to see things in terms of dichotomy, awareness of a lived body as the locus of the true self has been transmitted since time immemorial.[5])

Zen practice offers a direct way to overcome this oppositional way of understanding the self and body. We are invited to sit still and experience our body-mind in dynamic unity, with every here and now breath. Thus we are opened to experience what Dogen refers to as "dropping off our body-mind"—and dropping off the body-mind of "other." This opens the door to an entirely new way of being—and a new way of seeing the self in all things and all things as the self.

This Very Body, The Great Wide Earth

In the practice of zazen, we are enjoined to set the mind in stillness, letting it be fully absorbed in the here and now by following every breath. As our practice deepens and we ripen in awareness, we are readied for the moment when ego-centered consciousness—and all its oppositions—disintegrate. Literally, our body-mind drops off as does the body-mind of Other. This is likened to the process of peeling an onion. But after peeling away layer after layer of an onion, in that tearful moment of reaching the core, what is left?

In this moment we realize our true self—which is no-self. This no-self is described in Buddhist texts by a series of negations. In the famous Heart Sutra, recited in Zen temples all over the world, it is said there is "no form, no sound, no odor, no taste, no object of touch, no image."

In this moment we arrive at the zero-point where all opposites merge; all positive and negative elements in our being and in the universe merge—and in merging, become fully transformed.[8] This zero-point moment places us at the fulcrum of the universe. From here we can move the world at will and "walk freely in the universe," as Wu-men wrote (in his poem introducing his collection of koans).[9]

It is from the zero-point perspective that the following exchange between two Zen monks takes place:

> *Officer Lu Cheng said to Nan-ch'üan, "Teaching Master Chao was quite extraordinary: he was able to say, 'Heaven and earth have the same root, myriad things are one body.'"*
> *Nan-ch'üan pointed to a peony in the garden, and said, "People today see this flower as in a dream."*[10]

Our ego-centered consciousness is unable to see things as they truly are; it perceives as a subjective self thought to be within. Thus, noted philosopher Immanuel Kant, we only see "things as they appear" *(phenomena)* and will never be able to grasp "things as they are" *(noumena)*. As Nan-ch'üan shows us, until the subject-object polarity of ego-centered consciousness is overcome, we can only "see this flower as in a dream"—in other words, we cannot see it as it really is.

From the zero-point perspective, we can say with master Chao, "Heaven and earth have the same root, myriad things are one body." These "myriad things" refer to each and every thing in the universe: mountains and rivers, the sun, moon and stars, this chair, table, and coffee cup. And we can exclaim with Hakuin: "This very body, the body of the Buddha"—not as a metaphysical statement, but as a pointer to awakening.

From this perspective, "this very body" is not just our physical body, in opposition to the physical bodies—and thus to all things—in the universe. As our mind's eye opens, "this very body" is no different from the mountains, rivers, sun, moon, and stars.

Hologram: The Part Is the Whole

The Zen enlightenment experience—the zero-point where "heaven and earth have the same root, myriad things are one body"—can be approached from a different angle.

I was made aware of a fascinating dimension of our bodiliness when I went back for a family visit to the Philippines some years ago. My youngest brother, a medical doctor, related to me his dilemmas in practicing medicine in the semi-rural, semi-urban area in the Philippines where he originally opened a clinic. The majority of those who came to him were from low-income families who could hardly pay for his services, let alone buy the medicines he was taught to prescribe by his Western medical training. It broke his heart to charge them even enough to meet his own family's upkeep. This led him to explore homeopathic healing and Chinese medical practices, including acupuncture.

After a while he became proficient in acupuncture and began to attract patients looking for this kind of treatment. For his poorer patients, acupuncture was a treatment that didn't require a great deal of money. But he also had a growing clientele of well-to-do persons who wanted acupuncture to help them lose weight. He told me how an acupuncture needle, applied to a certain place on the earlobes, caused a loss of appetite for a number of weeks. The overall effect was a loss of weight within a short period of time; with continued treatment, there could be a ten to twenty pound loss. Now he had financially rewarding practice that balanced his treatment of his less well-off patients.

This story of my brother's medical practice—and the fact that this model does indeed work—opened my eyes to the fascinating view of the human body that the Chinese had been putting into practice for thousands of years. Healing was based on the interconnectedness of our various body parts and their proper stimulation.

The ear, for example, is a minuscule model of the body as a whole, with each part of the ear corresponding to parts of that whole body. Likewise the soles of the feet and palms of the hand contain, in a very concrete and tangible way, the whole body. Without going into detail, we can summarize these new vistas now being opened to science with the word *hologram*.

The term hologram is taken from lensless photography. It refers to an image whose every part, when enlarged, can be shown to contain the whole. If a holographic picture of a mountain, for example, is cut into sections, each section will show not just a part of the mountain, but the whole mountain. In short, each part contains the whole, completely and without deficiency.

Another direction of scientific research illustrates our point:

the work of Karl Pribram, the Stanford neuroscientist whose research into the human brain led to some startling perspectives. This work has been seen to complement the work of physicist David Bohm. Their findings in neurobiology and physics, respectively, point to an understanding of the human brain—and of the whole universe—as a hologram. In short, each part of our brain (as seen in the work of Pribram) and each part of this universe (as seen in the work of Bohm) contains the whole.[11]

These may seem like startling statements indeed, difficult to fathom. They are statements that ask us to look at the whole picture from a different vantage point. But this new perspective is not a novel one at all. It has been opened to all those who, through various meditative practices, arrived at the zero-point. Ancient Hindu and Buddhist texts are full of descriptions issuing forth from this perspective.

The Jewel Net of Indra is one such image of interconnectedness. This is a net of interconnected jewels wherein each jewel fully reflects all the others. In China this was developed and expounded in Hua Yen Buddhism, deriving inspiration from a sutra of the same name.[12]

Surprisingly enough, we find imagery of this same notion in traditional Christianity: the doctrine of the Mystical Body of Christ.

The Mystical Body of Christ

The description of the universe as a hologram, wherein every part contains the whole, is the very image given in the traditional Christian doctrine on the Eucharistic bread as the Body of Christ.

I recall my catechism teacher explaining to us children that the round wafer was the real Body of Christ, and that each one was the fullness of the same Christ. We were reassured that whether we received a whole round host or half of a host—sometimes the priest would divide the hosts so there would be enough to go around—each piece was in itself the full Body of Christ. At that time, it was only by simple (blind) faith that I was able to accept the fullness of Christ in each piece of the Eucharistic bread.

I also recall an instance at San-un Zendo, where a Christian member of our Zen community was trying to explain the Eucharist to Yamada Roshi over tea after a Zen sitting session. (Yamada Roshi had been receiving many Christians as his Zen disciples since the early 1970s. And during Zen retreats, he had permitted them to have their own eucharistic celebration in another room, while the Buddhists were chanting the morning sutras in the main Zen hall.)

This Christian practitioner expressed very simply to the group: "We Christians believe that the bread offered in the Eucharist is the real Body of Christ." Whereupon Yamada Roshi—without the least bit of surprise or doubt—replied, "Of course!"

In other words, from his enlightened perspective, he could see and understand clearly (indeed much more clearly than many Christians) the reality of the Real Presence in the Eucharistic bread. The enlightened eye is not so much a special or esoteric way of seeing, accessible only to a few. It is a way of seeing that overcomes the subject-object dichotomy. It is a way of seeing things as they really are.

This way of seeing is open to all, when the veil caused by the dualistic habit of mind is lifted. Lifting this veil is precisely what Zen practice about. By quieting the dualistic mind and enabling it to rest upon the zero-point, things can be seen in their true and original light.

In a meditative way, we can take the hint from the Christian celebration of the Eucharist. Then we may get a glimmer of the new heaven and new earth that we are invited to enter. Let us put ourselves in the context of a Eucharistic celebration, at this point, and follow its steps.

We might begin by simply placing our gaze on the bread and the wine that are offered in the celebration. Then take it from there. First of all, where does this bread come from, and whence the wine? Here we might trace the elements before us right to their source: to the wheat growing in the fields, the grapes dangling from the vines.

The wheat and the grapes are connected to earth through their stalks and vines, respectively. They are nourished in the bosom of this great wide Earth, with its rich soil full of minerals and natural nutrients, and where all sorts of living beings—bacteria, earthworms, and so many more—also thrive and contribute to the nurturing of life. Rain falling from the clouds waters the Earth, letting its nutrients flow through the roots of the plants. The plants are also nourished by the sun, whose energy is poured into the green leaves for the process of photosynthesis. In the process, plants return oxygen to the atmosphere, which numerous animal species need for their own life process, in a constant balance of give and take.

We can also see the work of countless human hands, in this process of bringing the wheat and grapes to this table in the form of bread and wine. There are the rough hands that tended the soil, the caring hands of their spouses, the little hands of their children. There are the hands of the laborers in the mills, wine presses, and packing factories; and the hands of the truck drivers and their families at home waiting for their return; and the hands of the storekeepers and their employees, struggling to manage on meager incomes.

The fruits of the labor of the whole human community are right here, in this bread and wine prepared for the offering. The prayer of the community echoes these interconnections quite pointedly: "Blessed are you, God of all creation. Through Your goodness we have this bread and wine to offer. Fruits of the earth, the work of human hands."

In and through this single piece of bread and one cup of wine, we are offered the whole interconnected network that led up to it—the whole of God's creation. It is in this totality right here before us, as we prepare for the pronouncement of those sacred words: "This is my body, given for you."

This offering, made in this particular time and place, is not limited to the circumstantial here and now. "Do this in remembrance of me," Christ tells us. In other words, it re-collects, re-enacts, re-lives an event that happened around two thousand years ago. Somewhere in Palestine, Jesus offered the bread and cup to his disciples, signifying the offering of himself in obedience to the Father, an obedience that would lead him to death on the cross. With that death came a new life, the life of the Risen Christ that now fills the universe.

The Eucharistic celebration is a re-enactment, a re-actualization, of Christ's offering of his whole being to God. It re-presents a primal event that cuts through all of history and gives it meaning. When we take up the bread and wine and offer it in thanksgiving to the Source of all creation, we put ourselves in a dimension that cuts through time to "before the foundation of the world" (Eph. 1:4), and space, through "all things in heaven and all things on earth" (Eph. 1:10).

Participating in this primal event brings the meaning of our being fully to light: "This is my body, given for you": These words take us through time and space to the here and now. Here we partake in the newness of life and, to those "with eyes that see," discover the very secret of the universe.

"This is my body, given for you": The bread and wine is not just to be gazed at, but consumed and dissolved into the communicant's body in Eucharistic celebration. Receiving the bread and wine, the words "This is my body, given for you" resonate more intimately. The bread and wine is the whole of creation. All this is offered in thanksgiving to the Source of creation—in and through Jesus' life, lived in total obedience even to death on the cross.

Each Eucharistic celebration is an invitation to behold the

cosmic dimensions of what is right in front of us. It can be our passage to mystic depths as we open ourselves to the experience of "this very body" in its cosmic dimensions. At the same time, by bringing us back down to Earth, it puts us in touch with the concrete realities of this broken body that is Earth itself.

The Body Broken

In the Roman Catholic rite, participants are invited to turn to one another for the greeting of peace just before the reception of communion. In some Methodist churches, this greeting of peace is sometimes shared just after communion. Regardless of when it is shared, the greeting of peace is meant to remind the community that the Body we partake of—though eternally whole and undivided at its source—is still in a state of brokenness in this actual historical condition in which we find ourselves. Thus there is still need for reconciliation and healing.

At this point I would like to relate a powerful experience that brought home to me, in a very concrete way, all the dimensions of the Body. I was privileged to partake in a Eucharist service held in Perkins Chapel, at the seminary where I currently teach. This service was held in memory of the martyrs for justice in Central America.

As participants went up to the altar to receive the communion bread ("This is my body, given for you"), a deacon standing beside the communion minister handed each of us a small wooden cross to bring back to our pews. Each cross, made out of two popsicle sticks pasted one across the other, bore a small slip of paper. And on each slip was written a name, country, and date. On mine was the small inscription: *Victoria de la Roca, Guatemala, Jan. 6, 1982.*

After we were all settled back in our pews and after the usual momentary silence, we were invited to stand up one after another and, holding the small wooden cross up high with the right hand, to recite the name of the person written on the slip of paper, saying, "Presente!" after the name.

This was indeed an event that cut through barriers of time and space. One after another we stood up, cross uplifted, reciting, "Victoria de la Roca, Presente!" "Jose Bernardo, Presente!" "Estrella Consolacion, Presente!" Each name resounded throughout the congregation, with the proclamation, "Presente!"—and within all of us, with each name, were the words "This is my body, given for you."

With this the Communion of Saints became a living reality, in the very here and now. In this very body, "Presente!" Throughout all time and all space, "Presente!" And in this, too, was the tearful realization of all the hurt, sorrow, injustice, and brokenness still a painful reality in this real world of ours and in the lives of our fellow beings. The wounds of the martyred ones, named and unnamed, remain open in this Body, crying out for healing.

In that moment of "Presente!" images of men and women, young and old, still living or already deceased came vividly before me. There were those I had met on visits to my own country, the Philippines, struggling for their very survival, in situations similar to those in the grass-roots communities in Central and Latin America. Here were all their struggles, wounds, and tears, as well as their hopes and joys and laughter. "Presente!" And here was every sentient being in this universe, past, present, and future. "Presente!"

As my eyes opened to all the dimensions of "Presente," I could see in this very body the wounds of the whole Body. These wounds cry for healing: the millions of malnourished children, destined to die before the age of five; all the victims of physical violence wrought by human beings upon one another; and the wounds of countless other species and of Earth itself, caused through human greed, anger, and ignorance.

These wounds wreak havoc on individuals, on families, on ethnic communities, on the whole Earth-community itself. But—

while they have been with us throughout our history—in this century they have reached the stage of wounded-unto-death.

Awareness of our global woundedness and the realization that we carry these wounds in our very body empowers us to offer this very body for the healing of the whole. In what concrete way can I, as one individual, do this? Our response is based on how we see our connectedness to and our place within the whole Body.

Rekindling after "Burnout"

We are exposed to our common woundedness through our own individual wounds and those of our fellow beings. Seeing the global proportions of this woundedness, we may be tempted by a sense of powerlessness in the face of it all: "What can I do in a situation that is so immense, complicated, and deeply embedded in structures that have been there for ages?"

We may start with a sense of determination, aspiring to be an agent of healing through some form of social service, volunteer activity, engaged career, or way of life. But at some point we may experience what is commonly termed "burnout." This is a state of mind in which we—wanting only to be of service to others in our common woundedness—become overpowered by it all. In the process, we run out of steam and become disabled by this life of service, at which point we needing to withdraw for a time (or even entirely).

Zealous individuals who begin with selfless dedication to the task of healing of Earth's wounds, and who sacrifice a great deal of personal gain, comfort, or worldly success are especially liable to burnout. After applying themselves vigorously, they often conclude the situation is not getting any better, indeed, it may seem to be getting worse. Soon they ask: "What concrete result has come of all this work of mine? What have I made all these sacrifices for?" The sense of injustice, or sense of solidarity with our fellow beings in situations of oppression and suffering, which inspired us to become agents of healing or champions of justice, gradually turns into a sense of powerlessness or defeat. We are unable to give any further.

Behind such an experience, we can point to a subtle but very real and deep-seated attachment. Seen fully, it is attachment to the "I" that wants to see "results," a clinging to the "good" self that made so many sacrifices for "others." Naturally we expect something good to come out of all this. But the "I" that wants results and sees itself as "good" loses steam when it doesn't get what it wants. This "I" then loses confidence in its own "goodness."

Now this "I" is called upon to *let go*. Admit to powerlessness, inefficacy, and even defeat. The good "I" that expects good results from its endeavors is the final vestige of our delusive self-image— and the thin film it creates is preventing us from realizing the interconnectedness of our true self. It is only by letting go of that which is most precious to us—this sense of our own goodness and good results—that we can be truly free. By letting go of this delusive self-image, we can recognize in our powerlessness and defeat our *no-thingness*. Only then can we truly hear, in the depths of our being, the words "This is my body, given for you"—and see our true, universally interconnected self.

This simple "letting go," however, cannot be achieved through our own efforts. Because, in those moments of feeling overwhelmed with a sense of powerlessness, we are powerless to even let go. We either cling desperately to what we have left or wallow in our debilitating and disturbing—yet somewhat snug and numb—inability to offer another hand to anybody or take another step forward.

We are tempted to settle into this snug, numb, cozy feeling, in a dazed state approaching suspended animation, unable to do anything for months or even years. It would make all the difference in the world if, before yielding to this temptation, we were to step back and take stock of ourselves. See what is happening to us. This is where Zen practice can be invaluable.

A moment of awareness of our utter powerlessness and no-thingness—when the only thing left "to do" is simply "to be" and admit it and accept it—can be the greatest turning point of our life. Simply "to be," shorn of all power "to do," places us at rock-bottom. At rock-bottom of what we are, there is no trace of self-construct to bank upon or cling to. There is only pure being, stripped of all "doing" and "having." In this state of total naked-ness, what we are left with is simply "this very body"—breathing in, breathing out. Breathing in, breathing out.

It is here that things can take a totally revolutionary turn. Sim-ply being this body, breathing in and out, we abandon ourselves totally, in each moment, to the mystery of that Breath. Then its healing power can take over in us and become the balm for our woundedness and brokenness. In Zen terms, settling into this basic state of being is called *shikan taza,* or "just sitting."

Bereft of all doing and having, simply being—this totally naked, totally emptied self disposes us to the full impact of the words "This is my body, given for you." It is only this revelation—and not our own efforts—that can rekindle us. This gratuitous and pure work of grace, waiting for us all along in the Breath, can rekindle our burnout, renew our energy, and give us the power to heal this body, the Earth, in its woundedness and its wholeness.

Just as in the beginning the Breath moved over the waters giv-ing everything its form, shape, and being, this same Breath now blows over the dying embers of our wounded body, rekindling the fire within us that will renew the face of Earth.

7

Coming Home—
A Six-Point Recovery

W<small>E HAVE NOW</small> seen various aspects of the Zen way of life: its basic suppositions and fruits, the structure of practice centered on the Breath, the experience of enlightenment in discoverying the true self, the flowering of that experience in enhanced awareness of the mystery of ordinary life, and the opening to a vision of interconnectedness with everything realized as *this very body.*

We have also seen how these themes resonate with the Good News of Jesus, allowing the Christian practitioner to experientially appropriate this message and embody it in daily life.

By spelling out these connections more explicitly, we can now bring this message to bear on the healing of our Earth community. How does Zen practice, and the way of life flowing from it, address the healing of alienated human beings caught in the trap of the separative I-consciousness?

In Chapter 1, we traced the root cause of our woundedness to this. The I-consciousness at the helm of our day-to-day life draws a distinct line of separation between "I" as subject and everything else, separating us from the natural world and our fellow human beings by viewing them as "other," or objects out there.

By building up an idealized image of "I" we become Other to ourselves, alienated within our own being, as it were, by "six degrees of separation." As long as we are confined by this I-consciousness, we live in opposition to—and therefore inflict wounds upon—nature, our fellow humans, and ourselves. We can see this in our personal life, our work life, and the various social groups we identify with, which serve as our "extended ego." Feeling threatened from all sides, we live with constant insecurity.

We are also overtaken by a sense of cosmic separateness. This sense of displacement and homelessness is an anxiety that manifests in various ways. It urges us to implore, with Hui-k'o, the Second Zen Ancestor in China: "My mind is not yet at peace. I beg you, please give it peace."

In preceding chapters, we have seen that the Zen experience of awakening enables us to break through the delusive framework that prevents us from seeing things as they truly are. This breakthrough enables us to overcome cosmic separateness and displacement; and to see, in a very concrete way, our place in the universe—and our intimate connectedness with it. It reveals our true, integral self.

Zen awakening is an experience of *coming home* to our true self. Having overcome the illusory barriers set up by separative I-consciousness, we have a deep sense of at-home-ness. We are at home in the cosmos, at home with our fellow humans and all living beings, and at home with the Earth. We realize that we have always been "at home." We were never separated or displaced. Yet it is only now that, to paraphrase T.S. Eliot, we know it for the first time.

In Christian terminology, all the time we thought we were lost in a state of sin, yet through it all God was with us. The awakening experience enables us to proclaim with a sense of gratitude that amazing grace wherein we are found and brought home. Like the loving father in the story of the prodigal son (Luke 15:11–32), God was always there waiting, until we were ready to come home. When we finally do, there is endless celebration in the household.

The Zen life leads to and, conversely, flows from this deep sense of cosmic at-home-ness, wherein we recover everything we thought we were separated from. The word *recovery* implies both the retrieval of something lost and a return to the state of well-being and wholeness that was our original state. This state of holiness and blessedness was there "even before the foundation of the world" (Eph.1:4).

Reflecting on the various dimensions of *coming home* to our true, integral self we recognize a six-point recovery: (1) recovery of the *now*, (2) recovery of the *body*, (3) recovery of our *shadow*, (4) recovery of the *feminine*, (5) the recovery of *nature*, and (6) the recovery of our *neighbor*. Each of these is a vital dimension of our true self. This six-point recovery is an overcoming of the six degrees of separation described in Chapter 1 as we traced the roots of our woundedness.

Let us look at these six interrelated dimensions of our healing.

Recovering the Now

As we have seen in the previous chapters, the spirituality and way of life that blossoms from Zen practice can be described simply as a way of *living fully in the here and now*. Zen spirituality paves the way for our recovery of life that is actually lived in the reality of each present moment. It implies a recovery from a life in pursuit of some ideal of happiness or fulfillment projected somewhere "out there" in the future. Instead, we are made fully aware of the mystery of the present.

An example of this is given by Thich Nhat Hanh in his book *The Miracle of Mindfulness.* Explaining what he means by the key term "mindfulness," the author describes two ways of washing dishes: we can wash dishes to get them clean or simply to wash dishes.[1] Our ordinary consciousness says, "What else? Isn't that why we wash dishes, to get them clean?" It seems preposterous to question that.

In the same vein, we tend our gardens so beautiful flowers come up in the spring; so our neighbors can see them and say, "Oh, what nice flowers you have." And we take the bus or train or drive our car to work, so we can get there and do our job. Then we can earn money to support our family, so the children can go to good schools, so they can get good jobs and start their own families, so we can all live happily ever after. And so on with everything else in our life.

We take it for granted that this is "normal" life. This is what everybody else does, propelled by the sense of purpose or goal that we expressed in our attitude toward washing dishes: we wash dishes *to get them clean.* We get them clean so we can go on to the next thing, like going to the living room to watch television, and then get ready for bed so we can get enough energy to get us through the next day's work.

Our human lives seem to be constantly in pursuit of some purpose or goal that we ourselves or someone else may have set for us. We have long-term goals, such as making a great deal of money, becoming famous, achieving success on the corporate ladder, or just working long enough so we can payoff the mortgage and get the kids through college. And we have short-term goals, such as getting the dishes clean so we can get them out of the way, so we can relax, so we can prepare for the next day's job, so we can keep bread on the table . . . and so on.

We can say this is all a consequence of being conditioned by time, viewed as a linear movement in a fleeting present that recedes into the past and rapidly moves toward the future. This time-conditioned nature prods us to look to the future for something better than our present. There we will fulfill our hopes, attain our goals, complete our projects; and there, we imagine, lies the key to the happiness we so long for. If we exert ourselves now, our efforts will yield due results in the future.

No one questions this fundamental principle of human action. We enkindle our hopes for the future to motivate our life in the present. Thus we value things based on how well they serve our purposes and meet our future goals. We place a premium on things that get the job done—with less input of time and energy and with better results. Then we will have extra time and energy to do *other things* that bring about increased productivity.

And we treat others in a similar manner. Those who help us meet our goals are preferred. Our human relations then are governed by a principle of goal-centered selectivity.

We can only characterize a life in which everything is done for the sake of something other than itself as a state of alienation from life itself. The fact is, we have become deluded into thinking this is the only way we can live life: bound in time and space as we are, continuously looking to the future. Perhaps when we retire and have no external constraints of work and wage-earning, we will find relief from this frenzied life. But when we reach that point, we find ourselves bored, and dislocated. We then spend our time looking back on it all, asking ourselves what we might have missed.

Going through life each day, propped up by some imagined ideal of fulfillment in the future or in a glorious past gone by, we hardly notice how outside of life we are. Unless, of course, the weight of it all gets the better of us and we experience a crisis or breakdown. Then we're confronted with the question, "What is all this about, anyway?" What is behind our lack of inner peace, our sense of meaninglessness and frustration—not to mention the neuroses and mental imbalance that plague us and so many of our contemporaries?

It is when we are confronted with such questions and we step back to reflect on our situation that Zen can open a new door for us. It invites us to a way of life that takes life where it is, just as it is—and not other than that—beginning with simple, day-to-day things like washing the dishes.

Zen practice is centered on sitting meditation. We simply sit still and follow every breath. This enables us to come back to where the fullness of life awaits us: in the here and now. Every breath is lived in its fullness. Every sip of tea is relished. Every step is taken without worrying about the steps ahead; our whole being is placed on *this* step. Our awareness is fully in the here and now—in each moment and throughout our life. Yes, this is your life, right here, right now. This is our life with the recovery of *now*.

The Gospel message proclaimed by Jesus is no less an invitation to the recovery of the present moment. "The time is fulfilled. The reign of God is at hand" (Mark 1:15). It is an invitation to open our being and welcome this reign and all that it implies: the totality of our lives, beginning right here and now. In the very ordinary events of day-to-day life, we open our eyes and our whole being to the reality of God's active presence in all this. "The reign of God is in your midst" (Luke 17:21).

Just as Jesus embodied in his life the "reign of God" in all that he said and did, those of us who hear his message are called to embody that reign in our lives. From moment to moment, "follow me" right [into this present moment].

Jesus invites us to entrust our whole being to the reign of God and not worry about tomorrow: "Take no thought, saying, 'What shall we eat?' or 'What shall we drink?' or 'How shall we be clothed?' . . . seek first God's reign, and all these things shall be given to you" (Mt 6:31–33). We are invited to open to the discovery of the reign of God in every moment.

The famous scene of the Last Judgment (Mt 25:31ff) is also an important pointer to living in full awareness of the *now*. We may be easily led to take this passage literally, as something that will happen in a far distant future. But a closer look reveals something important. Those who are called to their eternal glory in God's reign are told "whenever you did this to one of these little ones, you did it to Me."

This passage is telling us to open our being to each and every one we encounter in life, and to respond accordingly with our whole being. Whether it's offering nourishment or solace, or providing an ear, or just saying "hello"—*in that very moment,* God's active presence is discernible. This is the Good News that Jesus proclaims: "In every moment I, myself, am knocking at your door. And when you open your being to Me in all these 'little ones,' I AM right there in your midst."

Unfortunately, as this message was handed down through the generations, it lost the sense of the impinging nature of God's reign in our lives. Christians tended to look for the fulfillment of that reign in an eschatologically far-distant future. Believing in the Christian Gospel came to mean belief in salvation in an afterlife. There, it is said, everything in this present life will find completion and fulfillment.

The belief in the Second Coming of Jesus the Christ as a future event tends to cloud his own assurance of his constant presence in our midst: "I will be with you always, till the close of the age" (Mt 28:20).

This is not to reject the Christian belief in the Second Coming as the culminating point of human history—in the same way we cannot and need not deny the phenomenon of time as a linear movement toward the future.

What Zen invites us to glimpse is that dimension that cuts through past, present, and future. This same dimension was experienced by the author of the letter to the Ephesians, writing in the same breath about the time "even . . . before the foundation of the world," as well as "the fullness of time" wherein all things will be united in Christ, "all things in heaven and things on earth" (Eph. 1:4,10). A glimpse of that fullness of time where past, present, and future come together is the zero-point, where the whole cosmos is united "in one head, Christ."

The doctrine of the Second Coming of Christ moves from an attitude of *banking* on (literally acquiring credits and debits for) a far-distant future, to a stance of constant vigilance in the *now*. Here, too, are implications of a dualistic view of Christian teaching, particularly the belief in an afterlife. Everything done in the here and now is seen merely as a means to an end; life on earth is seen as a piling up of merits and demerits, credits and debits, to be accounted for in the afterlife. This dualistic view is behind the criticism that Christianity offers "pie in the sky," thus numbing us to the tasks of the here and now.

By calling our attention back to the here and now, Zen practice enables us to recover the original impact of the Good News: the reign of God is already at hand, in our very midst, as we go about our many tasks of day-to-day life. We may continue doing exactly the same things we did before: washing dishes, going to work, and coming back home. But a Zen life is strikingly different from a life that banks on fulfillment in the future—in this or an after-life.

Without denying or neglecting our time-conditioned existence or rejecting the possibility of an afterlife, we can center ourselves in the here and now. We can discover the reign *already at hand*—even as it is *not yet*. Historically speaking, we may indeed be moving toward the complete manifestation of God's reign as promised. But we are called to live this very life at its source, to finds its glory and fullness in the here and now.[2] Zen invites us to a life that opens itself to the Holy One right in our midst.

When we wash the dishes, we simply wash dishes—which doesn't mean they do not get clean. Getting clean is the natural result of being truly able to wash dishes. So we enjoy the fruits of what we do, because we do what we do for its own sake. Placing our whole being in the here and now, we engage in our various tasks that this world demands of us. And we live to the full each moment along the way, not measuring our lives based on the results of what we do.

When we are not in a state of separation, driven by purposeful tasks, we can relish life as it is, take things as they are, feeling the warm water on our hands, our feet on the floor. We can open ourselves to the totality and mystery of life—with its ups and downs, joys and pains—right where we are.

A Zen expression says "Chop wood, carry water." Meet life in all its mystery and wonder right where you are. Chop wood, carry water—and lo and behold, things fall into place. The wood gets to the hearth, the water gets into the kettle, the fire is lit, and the rice gets cooked. And we partake of the rice, nourished and grateful.

Recovery of the *now* heals the fissure created by our time-bound pursuits of projected ideals. This fissure has impelled us to relate to our world as a means to our projected goals. This is what is behind our exploitative and utilitarian relationships. With the healing of this fissure and its attitudes, we can cherish and treasure our relationships and celebrate our being together in the here and now. Recovery of the *now* is thus vital to an ecologically sound way of life that enables us to value and celebrate our life on Earth.

Recovering the Body

The recovery of the *now* is crucial to the recovery of our body. Behind much of our brokenness and woundedness is our alienation from our own bodies. Recovery of *now* is the key to healing.

In Western Christendom, the body has often been looked down upon as a source of temptation that deflects the soul from its eternal destiny, as a source of evil weighing down on our efforts to do good. This dualistic view places the body in opposition to the soul. And it has led to an attitude of denigration of anything associated with bodily existence.

"If it gives pleasure, it must be sinful," goes a saying often uttered half-jokingly. But it strikes a chord in the experience of many raised in a traditional Christian atmosphere. Raised as a Roman Catholic in pre-Vatican II times, I remember those printed cards placed in the pews in church on Saturday afternoons to help us prepare for confession, enumerating the sins of the body, or better, sins *because of* the body. There were directives regarding the sins of the body and warnings of eternal damnation due to those sins. This made it difficult not to feel a tremendous sense of guilt in just having been born in a body, with all its proclivities to sin.

To be a spiritual person in this context meant not concerning oneself with things of the body, and not giving in to gratification of the senses—the palate, eyes, sense of touch, sexual pleasure, and so on. Ideally, one kept the body in tow and the flesh mortified, so they would not weigh down the flight of the spirit to the divine.

St. Ignatius of Loyola, in his rules for the Society of Jesus, writes on the vow of chastity that each one should "strive to be as the angels."[3] This spiritual ideal represents centuries of Christian belief and practice. This baggage of human flesh diverts one from that ideal—and easily leads one to lament having been born as an embodied being.[4]

The disdain toward the body in Western Christendom was reinforced by the philosophical views that ushered in the modern era. The Cartesian framework drew a sharp line between mind and body as distinct entities making up the human mode of being. Such views are the underpinnings of Western culture. And they are at the root of much of our culture's dis-ease and neuroses.

(In contemporary culture, these are manifested in the reactionary "cult of the body," and the prevalence of body-development programs—a telling indication that many are eager to reclaim the body with a vengeance.)

It is only in the last century that Western philosophy has begun to overcome dualism and do justice to the embodiment of human existence, as the starting point for considering our very being.[5]

More recent philosophical and theological developments focus on bodiliness to overcome the dualistic views of the past.[6] Biblical scholarship has also called attention to more holistic views of the body in Hebrew Scriptures and New Testament writings prior to later dualistic developments influenced by Greek thought. The doctrine of the resurrection of the body, now receiving renewed attention, affirms the bodily dimension and the centrality of body in the Christian understanding of human existence. This distinguishes Christianity from other philosophical and religious worldviews that make the separation of body and spirit ultimate and unbridgeable.[7]

The Zen practice and way of life, with its enhanced appreciation of the sacredness of bodily being, awakens us to the cosmic and earthly dimensions of bodiliness. Recovery of the body is not merely theoretical; it is a lived experience, in our concrete, historical, day-to-day life.[8]

With the body as the locus of Zen awakening, meticulous care is given to posture. We then focus our whole being on the breath. Mindfulness is brought to every breath and step and to every aspect of our day-to-day life. Thus we experience our body, in its manifold dimensions, to the fullest. In this very body—*"this very body, the body of the Awakened One"*—we connect with the ultimate dimension of our being.[9]

By coming home to my own body as my true self, I am at home in the universe. This realization opens our eyes to the grandeur and mystery of bodiliness. It enables us to celebrate our body as *that which makes us what we are in our relatedness to everything in the universe.*

This very body is the locus of the universe. The universe is expressed concretely in everything we experience as body—from the moment we wake up, through our activities of the day, and as we sleep at night. The interconnectedness of the universe is manifest in this very body, a wondrous and unrepeatable configuration of Earth and stardust, given fresh new life with every breath.

Becoming a parent is a vivid experience of our interconnectedness with the throb of life. To gaze at our newborn infant, born from a loving body-to-body union with our beloved, fills us with a tremendous sense of awe. *In this very body* flows unfathomable life and power that can bring about the birth of this delicate new being—a being who embodies this same mystery. This unfathomable life and power has coursed through countless generations, connecting our every heartbeat with the heartbeats of all who have gone before.

The natural awe we feel in face of the mystery of life needs no special effort to conjure; it can only be enhanced and deepened. The Zen awakening experience opens us to such depths. Here we can embrace each and every sentient being as *this very body.* And we can say that we are truly the mother of every child and the child of every mother.

The recovery of the body through Zen practice overcomes the false dichotomy between mind and body that has shaped much of Western culture. By re-appropriating our bodiliness as the locus of our true self, it also overcomes the gap between our own body and each and every other body. Thus the pain of every sentient being in the universe is felt as my own, *in this very body.* This naturally draws us to engage in tasks toward its healing, in all the ways we can.

Recovering Our Shadow

A dimension of our existence to which depth psychologists call our attention is the "shadow." This "dark side" of our being is the one we would rather not see. Buried in our unconscious, it is everything we would describe as negative, destructive, violent, chaotic, or evil.[10]

The interplay of polar opposites that make up our worldly existence abounds: good and evil, beautiful and ugly, pleasant and unpleasant, creative and destructive, light and dark, life and death. In the face of this, the egoic self—the standpoint from which we view the world—places itself on the side of the good, beautiful, pleasant, creative, light, and life, and rejects the other side.

With this egoic self, or separative I-consciousness at the center of our personality (from *persona,* or mask, in Latin), we are continually idealizing ourselves and therefore identifying with one—while denying or dissociating from the other side of our own being. We do this using the mechanisms of *suppression or repression.* Suppression is the "deliberate elimination by the separative consciousness of all those characteristics and tendencies in the personality that are out of harmony" with that which we value as positive. Repression is simply allowing those negative aspects to fade into the background and out of our consciousness.

However, by dis-identifying or denying the negative side of these polar opposites, the I-consciousness creates a rift at the core of our being. This paves the way for these negatives to "lead an active underground life of their own, with disastrous results" for both the individual and the community.[11] In other words, the suppressed or repressed polarities gather momentum and come to the fore with a vengeance, wreaking havoc on the individual as well as on society.

This bipolar nature of our existence as presented by depth psychology is dramatically portrayed in the story of Dr. Jekyll and Mr. Hyde. The good and evil sides of the same person find themselves acting out on different planes, unbeknownst to each other—manifesting what is known as a "split" personality. The unrecognized shadow remains active, undermining the good and bright side. We see how this actually works when outwardly respected persons are revealed to have skeletons hidden in the closets of their personal lives.

Further, we see how persons deemed to be good and upright citizens or church members, or leaders of the sangha or practice community, acting as the conscience of the community, can also be the most vindictive, judgmental, and cruel toward those who seemingly fall short of their moral standards. Such vindictiveness, judgmental mindset, and cruelty, depth psychologists would point out, come out of their vigorous efforts to deny their shadow side, which they then project on others. "Scapegoating" is one mechanism we humans use to deal with our shadow side by laying blame on some identifiable culprit—individual or group or type.[12]

On a grander scale, denial of our shadow side has resulted in hideous episodes of human history: innumerable wars fought in the name of some rightful cause; the Crusades, with their holy fervor to destroy the infidel; the Inquisition, with its religiously and legally sanctioned persecution of those who threatened the belief system of the established majority. In the last century, the Shoah, Hiroshima, Vietnam, the Killing Fields of Cambodia, Gulag, Tiennamen, Sarajevo—all are salient examples of the horrors we humans perpetrate in the name of some dazzling ideal.

In pursuit of such ideals, the delusive consciousness attempts to identify with the "good"—be it a "superior" humanity, a quick way to peace, democracy, equality, order, ethnic purity, or what have you—by suppressing or repressing its opposite and projecting it on the Other.

Going further, we can see how the twentieth-century worship of progress has resulted in our current global ecological crisis. Flanked by its powerful ministers, "science" and "technology," progress stands for all that is good and is uncritically identified with our happiness. Our pursuit of it, however, totally fails to consider its destructive toll on the Earth.

And so a rift opens at the core of our being, as we pursue an idealized "good" in a way that denies the shadow side of our existence. This rift comes to haunt us in the abhorrent events in our individual and communal history. It manifests itself in the brokenness and woundedness of the different dimensions of our being.

As long as the *I-me-mine* controls our lives, we are trapped in self-idealization. Seeing only the good, beautiful, bright side of our being, we fail to see the opposite pole. We look the other way, wish it away—or worse, suppress or repress it.

Denial of our shadow is the inevitable outcome of letting the separative I-consciousness have its way—not only in ourselves, individually, but also in the larger ethnic, financial, neighborhood, national, and corporate groups we identify with. Here it takes the attitude of "us versus them": we are on the side of the good; they are "the enemy."

We can see how this leads to the perpetual conflicts we find ourselves in. Whether on the individual or corporate level, the separative I-consciousness projects its shadow onto the Other "out there," where it fights it—thus contributing to its own destruction.

In considering our shadow, the problem we confront with the impending fact of our death is significant. Death looms as a constant threat to our being. Attempting to assert our being in the face of the nothingness we associate with impending death, we embark on all kinds of projects to continue our existence.[13] However, projects issuing from the denial of death are no more than desperate efforts to shield our ego from its shadow. This effort—we could call it an "edifice complex"—drives us to build all kinds of makeshift shelters for our threatened or wounded ego, and supports to prop it up.

Healing that wounded ego, however, does not come from continued efforts to shield it from the reality of the shadow. It comes from bringing ego face-to-face with this dark dimension of our being. We are called to confront our shadow: looking death in the face, for example, is the only way to learn how to live with it and not be threatened by it. To paraphrase the words of the Jesus character in the musical *Jesus Christ Superstar,* "To conquer death, you only have to die . . . you only have to die."

The recognition of and reconciliation with our shadow is crucial to our healing. Recognition and reconciliation involve first being able to *see* that there is a shadow side of our being, and then being able to *accept* it as part of us. Only by recognizing and accepting our shadow side can we become whole, integrated, and reconciled—and therefore truly and fully ourselves.

Of course, this does not mean giving in to the power of our negativity and destructiveness. When we let negativity have sway over us, we become agents of destruction, chaos, and death. It simply means breaking through the mask *(persona)* fabricated by our I-centered consciousness with its one-sided identity with our good and bright side. By allowing ourselves to listen to deeper dimensions of our being where the dark side lurks, we come face-to-face with the evil, chaotic, and destructive parts of our historical, communal, and personal existence. In the Zen practice of sitting meditation, we place ourselves fully in the here and now by following our breathing. This enables us to become more and more transparent to ourselves. As our practice ripens and we become more transparent to ourselves, we see through the I-consciousness to both the bright and the dark side of our being. We may then be surprised by a voice telling us—gently but clearly, with no room for doubt—*That thou art.*

Hearing that voice and all that it implies liberates us from our one-sided I-consciousness. It enables us to see in a new light, not only the good and beautiful, but also the evil, ugly, chaotic, and destructive. Seeing that these are inevitable and inseparable parts of us enables us to take responsibility for them.

Owning my shadow and taking responsibility for it paves the way for me to integrate it with the rest of myself, thus enabling me to come to wholeness.

In many communities of Zen practice, the Verse of Purification is recited regularly:

All harmful karma ever committed by me since of old,
on account of my beginningless greed, anger, and ignorance,
born of my body, mouth, and consciousness,
now I atone it all.

The recitation of this verse is an expression of our recognition, and acknowledgment, of all the evil in the world as also part of and caused by ourselves. "Atoning" for this evil is recognizing oneself as "at-one" with this evil and its harmful effects on myself and the rest of the world. And in so doing, we take responsibility for it, and live accordingly, accepting the consequences, but also seeking to transform them in the direction of what is less harmful and more beneficial, for myself and for everyone.

As we deepen in our Zen practice, we can reach down to the depths of our true self and touch that point where our bright and dark sides meet. Here we meet our shadow squarely, without opposing or resisting it. Simply recognizing and owning it, we take responsibility for it and face the consequences with equanimity. At this point there is no more fear. Having reached the realm beyond light and dark, life and death, we find ourselves in the fullness of freedom.[14]

The Christian doctrine of Christ's descent into hell, often glossed over or played down, in this context indicates his encounter and reconciliation with the shadow aspect of cosmic existence. Zen practice can help us appreciate this doctrine experientially, as we follow Christ in his descent to the netherworld of our being. This descent into hell is a condition for the Risen Christ to be a truly integrative power, reconciling the principalities and powers and all the warring opposites in the universe, uniting all "things in heaven and things on Earth" (Eph. 1:11).

This healing message of the Gospel is also expressed in the phrase: "The glory of God is the whole human being fully alive."[15] A whole human being, fully alive, is one who integrates the light and shadow sides of his or her being and thus comes to salvation, wholeness, and holiness.

Recovering the Feminine

It has been pointed out by many writers that our prevailing human civilizations have historically operated on the principles of subjugation, exploitation, dominance, and violence. History is witness to the pattern of dominance by humans over nature, by stronger tribes over weaker, by men over women. *Patriarchy* is the term that describes a mode of being and relating based on such principles. It is expressed through the human attitudes, actions, and institutions that shape our lives.[16]

These attitudes also lie behind our brokenness and woundedness. This is a mind-set that makes the *now* a mere stepping-stone, a means to a future end. It treats the *body* as separate from the mind and as something to be controlled and subjected to so-called higher faculties. It avoids the *shadow* side of life, denying its presence by suppressing or repressing it or projecting it onto others. And it regards *nature* as an external object to be mastered, tamed, and dominated.

We have already indicated how Zen can provide a way to liberate us from these attitudes. Now we will see how the Zen practice and way of life can liberate us from the attitudes and institutions characterized as "patriarchal." This is what Zen can contribute toward the recovery of the feminine dimension of our being—referring both to males and females, though in different ways.

The Zen way of life leads to and flows from the interconnectness of everything in this universe. Awakening to this unleashes the powers of cosmic compassion to be fully at work in us. This in turn opens us to a mode of being characterized by *connectedness* and *relationship,* rather than by control; by *cooperation* rather than by competition; by *partnership* rather than by dominance; by *nurturing and caring* rather than by subjugation and exploitation. The actualization of this mode of being in our personal lives, social structures, and institutions is what we mean by the recovery of the feminine.

To characterize these traits—connectedness, relationship, cooperation, partnership, nurturing, and caring—as traits of the feminine dimension does not imply that *maleness* is identified with their opposites. Nor does it imply that only women manifest these traits. This view, which derives from Jungian psychology, is often stereotyped and overextended but nevertheless useful. It suggests that regardless of gender, each one of us partakes of a masculine and a feminine dimension in our being. Our projected social character is then determined by which of these dimensions is more prominent in our relationships with one another. It is in this context that we contrast the "feminine" and "masculine" dimensions by the traits described above.

In the Buddhist tradition, the feminine dimension is given expression in the figure of *Kuan Yin* (Japanese, Kannon, short for

Kuan Shi Yin; and also in Japanese, Kanzeon, or "Hearer of the Sounds of the World"). Kuan Yin is the bodhisattva of cosmic compassion. She is shown as having a thousand arms that can reach in all directions to deliver sentient beings from their manifold forms of suffering.[17]

The figure of Kuan Yin points to a mode of being whereby— having been emptied of the delusive and divisive ego-centered consciousness and having realized the interconnectedness of all beings in the universe—one hears and in hearing *realizes oneness with* the sounds of the world: the cries of children dying of hunger, the plaint of mothers caring for those children; the voices of those silenced, imprisoned, and persecuted by the powerful of the world; the cries of the homeless, refugees, and those discriminated against; the cries of dolphins grieving the slaughter of their marine companions by thoughtless humans with so-called efficient fishing methods; the cries of thousands of species of sentient beings going extinct from year to year; the cries of the mountains and forests being denuded.

As our practice deepens, we encounter Kuan Yin not as an external object of veneration, but as the very embodiment of the cosmic compassion encompassing all of us. This is what makes us what we most truly are. The realization of this true self in Zen practice enables us to see in full transparency our interconnectedness with all sentient beings, and with the mountains and rivers of this great Earth. This realization is the embodiment of Kuan Yin in our very life. The turning word for the practitioner, for the one who hears the sounds of Earth, is this: *That thou art.*

In the Christian tradition, Mary the Mother of Jesus is seen as an embodiment of compassion. The figure of Mary at the foot of the Cross is enshrined in the Latin hymn *Stabat Mater,* "The Mother Stood By." Venerated for centuries, it is a figure that many turn to for help in time of need. Knowing suffering herself, she is able to listen to others with compassion and to intercede on their behalf. Her cosmic significance is described in the *Book of Revelations* as "a woman clothed with the sun . . . with child in the pangs of birth, in the anguish of delivery" (Rev. 12:1–6).

The theological significance of Mary is being given new attention, especially in light of discussions on the feminine dimension of divine compassion. In this context, a particularly suggestive theme is the image of Mary the Mother of God as the model of the church. Originally presented by St. Ambrose of Milan (339–397), this was taken up in the Second Vatican Council's *Document on the Church*.[18] This calls the church and its community, the hearers and proclaimers of the Gospel, to a mode of existence modeled on Mary the Mother of God, the compassionate one. Those of us who profess to be hearers of that Gospel are called to open our whole being to become like her, an embodiment of divine compassion. This is possible, not due to our own human efforts, but precisely insofar as we are emptied of our ego-centered consciousness. Insofar as, like Mary, we make our being transparent in a way that lets divine compassion work through us in our day-to-day life.

Letting go of the ego that wants to control, dominate, and possess, we can, like Mary, open and allow our being be overpowered by the Breath. Letting the breath take us where it will, we open totally to the power of cosmic compassion. Thus we open to the feminine side of the divine in the universe and let it guide us in the work of healing our wounded Earth.[19]

Recovering the Wonder in Nature

The ecological crisis impinging on us all and threatening the very survival of coming generations is greatly due to our distorted human attitude toward nature. The critical situation we now find ourselves in is rooted in this attitude of domination, a cosmological view that only serves our human desire for greater and greater control over nature.

The Christian (mis)reading of the Genesis story wherein man and woman are given the mandate to "subdue" and "have dominion" over other creatures (Gen. 1:28) has been noted as a key factor in this distorted worldview.[20] Within the Jewish and Christian traditions, attempts are being made to explain this story in terms of stewardship or the mandate to care for creation.[21] The significance, not to mention necessity, of such attempts is not to be gainsaid; but their efficacy remains to be seen in the actual way these individuals and communities are able to overcome a world-view based on human domination of nature. It remains to be seen if they will succeed in actually living out what many have called for as a new cosmology, founded on a vision of harmony and part-nership with nature.[22]

A new cosmology is a crying need—not only for those of us who continue to look to the Genesis story for an understanding of our place in the universe, but for all of us infected by the "mod-ern mentality" that separates humans from nature. Our critical situation, brought about by alienation from the natural world, confronts us as an urgent task that we need to address together as an Earth community.

Multilateral efforts at inter-religious dialogue can pave the way toward forging this new cosmology. From this may come a way of living and relating to nature that not only forestalls impending destruction, but also lead to a regeneration of Earth.[23]

From those with a theistic perspective, the contribution could be a view of our world and the entire universe as God's body.[24] This could, indeed, open the way for a different attitude toward the nat-ural world. Rather than treating it as a lifeless machine running on predetermined physical laws, we could regard nature as a sacred realm, throbbing with God's own life that nurtures our own.

The contribution that Zen makes toward the recovery of nature is more than a theoretical outlook. It is, first and foremost, a way of life that embodies our connectedness with nature in a concrete way. Those who do engage in Zen practice, and experience this connectedness with nature as an outcome, are especially called to express their experience. They are called to participate in the tasks of shaping a new cosmology—and living out its implications.[25]

Christians engaged in Zen practice are particularly invited to reread the Genesis story in light of their Zen experience. There are hermeneutical and theological issues to be brought into play, which we cannot go into here. But I will suggest one thread that can be pursued in such a rereading of Genesis from a Zen perspective.

Genesis 1:2 provides us with a very suggestive lead, as we read how "the Breath *(ruah)* of God was moving over the waters." This line is often passed over and not given much attention. But a Zen practitioner, aware of the centrality of Breath in forming our awareness of reality, will discover a deeply resonating chord in these words.

It is the primal Breath of God moving over the waters that gives shape and form to everything in this universe. In sitting practice, as we focus our attention on the simple process of breathing in and breathing out, the ego-centered consciousness is emptied. The terminus of this process is the *emptying* of both the "I" in here and the rest of the universe "out there." At this zero-point, there is *nothing but* the primal Breath, experienced in its full dynamic power. By simply breathing in and out, emptied of ego-centered consciousness, we touch the primal Reality that pervades the whole universe.

At this point let me recount the experience of a Catholic sister I was privileged to assist in an eight-day retreat. After several days of silence and breath awareness, she came to an interview with tears of joy and gratitude. She reported how during a walk in the garden she had "breathed the Breath of a flower." This momentary experience had opened up an entirely different perspective; it enabled her to see herself, her place in the universe, and her calling to the religious life in a new light. To make a long story short, she came in touch with the primal Breath in that encounter with a flower in the garden.

"Behold the lilies of the field" (Mt 6:28), Jesus enjoins us. Going beyond the theological or ethical lessons to be gleaned from the passage, we can take this as an invitation to simply *behold* the lilies of the field. Then, there may be something in store for us. In beholding the lilies of the field, we open ourselves to being touched at the core of our being. In so doing, we may find ourselves ushered into a new way of seeing not only the lilies, but everything else in the natural world and the universe as a whole. Sitting practice in Zen—breathing in and breathing out, emptying ourselves and surrendering to the power of the Breath—makes us susceptible to being touched at the core and transformed by that primal Breath that gives everything life.

The recovery of the wonder of nature that the Zen way of life leads to is based on a total surrender to that primal Breath. In letting the Breath be the guiding power in our lives, we realize in a very concrete way that every flower, every blade of grass, everything in the natural world is given being, as I am given being, in that Breath.

The recovery of our connectedness with the natural world does not imply that we humans will simply be passive spectators standing in awe and contemplating the natural processes around and within us. The recovery of nature, in this context, means that we recognize ourselves as part and parcel of nature itself; and we reclaim the right and responsibility to participate in the creative activity of the natural world.

Japanese Zen gardens are concrete examples of a way humans can reclaim their connectedness with nature and recover a sense of wonderment and awe. They express a sensitivity to the voices of nature that leads to a new creation in response to those voices.[26]

The Zen practice and way of life can make a vital contribution toward a new cosmology. It could ground us in a recovery of nature and in new modes of creation based on a sensitive listening to the voices of nature. As we repeatedly have seen in this book, the awakening experience at the heart of Zen opens our eyes to our interconnectedness with everything in this universe. It shows us our fundamental at-one-ness, not only with other human beings, but also with the "mountains and rivers and the great wide Earth"—as *this very body.*

To see the natural world as our own body radically changes our attitude toward it. The pain of Earth due to the violence being wrought upon it ceases to be something out there; it becomes our very own pain, crying out for redress and healing.

In Zen sitting, breathing in and breathing out, we are disposed to listen to the sounds of Earth from the depths of our being. The lament of the forests turning into barren desert, the plaint of the oceans continually being violated with toxic matter that poisons the life therein, the cries of the dolphins and fish come to be our very own cries.

Our response to these cries from the depths of our being will be guided by our concrete situation, from where we are and in the way we discern our role in the healing of the whole body.

Recovering and Reconnecting with My Neighbor

Awakening to my true, integral self brings the realization of my intimate interconnectedness with each and every one of my fellow human beings. I can no longer regard them as Other or as threats impinging on me, but precisely as my *neighbor.*

To be a neighbor is to be connected—not just by physical proximity, like the person living next door to me, but as someone in my immediate circle of care and concern. To acknowledge someone as my neighbor is to welcome that someone into my life in a way that my own well-being and destiny become connected with theirs.

In a well-known New Testament story (Luke 10:25–37), Jesus relates how three different persons, a priest, a legal expert, and a social outcast, come upon a wounded man, waylaid by robbers along the roadside. The first two, who were esteemed personages in the context of their time, find excuses to ignore the man and continue on their way. The third, an outcast, gets off his donkey, treats the wounded one, and brings him to an inn for further care. At the conclusion of the story, Jesus poses a question to his audience: "Which of these three, do you think, proved neighbor to the man who fell among the robbers?" (Luke 10:36).

In Christian tradition, beginning with the scriptural accounts handed down and reemphasized in the social teachings of the church since the last century, "love of neighbor" constitutes a central dimension of Christian life. It is put on the same plane as "love of God." These two central commandments, inherited from Jewish roots, define the Christian mode of being in the world.

The recovery of our neighbor, welcomed in love just as we love our own self, is therefore crucial to our return to wholeness, or *salvation*. For the Christian, this is clearly spelled out in the scene of the Last Judgment (Mt 25:31–46). Here the opening of one's life to other as our "neighbor" is manifest in these attitudes and acts: "I was hungry and you gave me to eat, I was thirsty and you gave me to drink, I was in prison and you visited me, I was alone and you comforted me." This love of neighbor is the pivotal point that opens us to the reign of God.

The centrality of our neighbor in an authentic life is also echoed in an oft-cited quotation: "I sought my soul, but my soul

I could not see. I sought my God, but my God eluded me. I sought my neighbor, and in the search, I found all three."

In Buddhist tradition, the realization of our interconnectedness with all beings, not limited to the human realm, is a central feature of the enlightenment experience. This has been a recurrent theme of this book: in our descriptions of the Zen experience, in its implications for self-understanding, and in the way it throws light on our life in the world. In the Loving-kindness *(Metta)* Sutta, we read: "May all beings be happy! As a mother regards her only child, have this mind in you toward all beings." This line gives us a glimpse into the mind of one who treads the path of awakening.

Metta is derived from the Sanskrit *maitri,* which means "friend," or "kin." The underlying implication of the passage is the recognition of all beings as *one's own kin,* and thereby belonging to one's intimate circle of care and concern. This indeed involves the expansion of one's circle, to embrace all beings in the universe: "weak or strong, tall, stout, medium, short, small, or large, seen or unseen, dwelling far or near, born or yet to be born."[27]

In short, the recovery of my neighbor is simply the opening of my eyes to this intimate connectedness with all beings, beginning with my fellow humans. In this awakening, I am able to overcome the separative I-consciousness: the one-dimensional, false and deluded self that is at the root of all the pain and suffering in the world. I am thereby able to realize and embody my true, integral self.

In conclusion, Zen spirituality ushers in a life characterized by the six-point recovery outlined above. This enables us to overcome the delusive self-image associated with the separative I-consciousness, and thus come home to our true self. The recovery of the *now* enables us to celebrate life where it is happening, here and now, and thus encounter the mystery of each moment. The recovery of our *body* enables us to live as a manifestation of the holy presence, a temple of the divine. The recovery of our *shadow* allows us to face the evil in the world with courage and equanimity and to take responsibility for it. And the recovery of the *feminine* is realized as we let go of that part of us that wants to control, dominate, and exploit; instead, to allow cosmic compassion to work in our being. Unleashing cosmic compassion effects our own healing; it also empowers us to participate in tasks of healing Earth. The recovery of the wonder of *nature* is linked with a heightened awareness of the sacramentality of the great wide Earth and everything in and on it. At the same time, we hear the cries of Earth, wounded and in pain, as our very own woundedness and pain.

Becoming whole within ourselves through these aspects of recovery, we recover and reconnect with our *neighbor*, who is welcomed as part and parcel of our own being and destiny.

This six-fold recovery takes place with our *coming home* to our true, all-embracing self. Ecology (based on the Greek *oikos*, or "home") is after all, no other than knowing and living in our own home. Zen awakens us to true knowing that enlightens our every thought, word, and action. Awakening to our true integral self, we realize we are at home—profoundly aware of our interconnectedness with everything in the cosmos. We are at peace, though we remain in pain with all sentient beings groaning in pain. We have never left home, yet come to know it for the very first time.

Epilogue:
Spirituality for Healing Our Global Society

IN THIS OPENING decade of the twenty-first century of the Common Era, we find our global society marked by stark contradictions that augur dark clouds over our communal future on this Earth.

On one hand, our successes in scientific research and information technology have given us an enormous amount of *knowledge* about the universe we live in.

On the other hand, seeing the scale of violence and turmoil that marked the twentieth century, and the continuing fractured and polarized state of our global society, we can only acknowledge that we have not been able to cultivate the genuine *wisdom* that would enable us to live in peace within ourselves and with one another on this Earth. Although we incessantly pursue *more* knowledge and acquire *more and more* information in all imaginable fields of inquiry, we also realize that this can never brings us inner peace and satisfaction, nor does it lead to wisdom or genuine happiness.[1]

On the one hand, our means of *communication* have developed to a point that what happens in one part of the globe can be transmitted to any other part almost instantaneously. The satellite televisions, broadband internet, and cell phones now accessible to the multitudes have facilitated communication over geographical distances.

On the other hand, the proliferation of these means of communication has not brought us closer to a sense of *communion* with one another, to an experience of being bonded in a community with living beings on Earth. On the contrary, speedy and readily accessible means of communication have only served to highlight our divisions and conflicts.

On the one hand, our technological advances have given us the *power* to send rockets to far-flung planets in our solar system, to generate nuclear energy, to massively exploit the Earth's natural resources, even to manipulate our natural processes to fit our human purposes.

On the other hand, never have so many of us felt such *powerlessness* before the behemoths of the overarching political, military, economic institutions and profit-driven conglomerates that dominate the global scene. There is a prevailing sense of the individual's powerlessness to make a difference in the directions our global society is heading. Many of us are led to a sense of near-desperation at our seeming inability to change how things are happening in the world. This sense of powerlessness pulls the rug of security from under the feet of individuals and groups in our globalized but fractured society.

This sense of powerlessness is heightened by the identity crisis felt by more and more of us, as we are stripped of our certitudes and watch the disintegration of longstanding traditions. More and more young people are driven to acts of destruction and terrorism; many others tend to seek a sense of consolidation and comfort by aligning themselves with those so-called leaders who offer clear-cut, either-or solutions to world problems. It is easy to place one's allegiance upon those who use forceful and persuasive words to issue blanket condemnations against "the enemy," pledging all-out war against "them."

The dramatic rise of incidents of violence in different parts of the world, on one hand, and the more stringent measures being imposed by political leaders and governments to tighten control over the populace, on the other—all serve to exacerbate a sense of insecurity felt by peoples throughout the world. This sense of insecurity generates a vicious cycle, whereby political regimes, with the backing of segments of the populace, are more prone to turn to drastic means and resort to military action in response to incidents of violence. People are led to think that they are being protected against "the enemy," and thus are deflected from the more truly pressing need to examine the deeper causes of that insecurity. All this only further highlights the contradictions, deepens the insecurities, and aggravates the suffering of increasing numbers of people in our world today.[2]

As we already know all too well from history and from current events, military measures only fan animosity and escalate conflict among those involved. Meanwhile, a handful of governments possess the kinds of weapons that can trigger massive destruction and murder, to the point of threatening the survival of our species on this Earth. In an increasingly tense global situation, the possibility that such weapons may in fact be used can unfortunately not be ruled out.

What we urgently need in our global society is the communal *wisdom* to see things as they are. This would enable us to direct our actions toward wholesome and life-giving rather than death-dealing directions. We need a sense of *communion* with one another, our fellow living beings on this Earth, to inspire us individually and collectively to attitudes and acts of genuine compassion, instead of acts and policies of exclusion and hostility generated by insecurity. We the people need a sense of *empowerment* to muster the courage to follow up these attitudes and acts of compassion in the public arena. This would transform not only our individual lives, but also the structures and institutions of our communal life as an interconnected global community.

The wisdom to see things as they are, a sense of communion that would support individual acts and public policies of caring and compassion, a sense of empowerment that would generate courage and energy in people like us to work toward the transformation of unjust and violent structures that cause our suffering— these are vital features of a spirituality that can heal our polarized and wounded global society.

Incidentally, there are dualistic kinds of "spirituality" based on the misconceived ideal of "detachment from the world," which many also turn to as a way of coping with the world's woundedness and apparent hopelessness. These merely provide people with an escape hatch from the world with all its contradictions and conflicts. Instead of being able to address our problems and grappling with them, these urge us to retreat into an "inner realm of the spirit," or set our eyes and hopes on some otherworldly dimension or afterlife.

True, genuinely integral and healing spirituality calls for a radical disengagement, but not from "the world" nor from "the body" or from "this earthly life" as such. Rather, a healing kind of spirituality calls us to detach ourselves from those *attitudes and actions* that heighten our divisions or tend to exacerbate conflict among us. While calling for a disengagement from such divisive attitudes and actions, at the same time, an integral spirituality also calls us to a thoroughgoing engagement with our earthly tasks, rather than an escape from them. Grounded in a vision of interconnectedness and compassion for all sentient beings, a healing spirituality cannot but be an *engaged* kind of spirituality that plunges itself right in the midst of the muddy waters of this world in working toward the well-being of all. It must never be an escapist spirituality that preaches dualistic detachment and disdain for the things of this world.

A healing spirituality can save us from a sense of powerlessness, and instead, enable us to discover a *source* of empowerment for transforming society. As we recover our true identity in realizing our interconnectedness with one another, we awaken to an expanded notion of Self that embraces the Other in reverence and love. This embracing attitude is the antidote to the temptation to retreat into alliances or subgroups that demarcate "us" against "them."

A healing spirituality is also enriched by inter-religious encounters. This means it cannot be the monopoly or prerogative of any one religious tradition, community, or institution. Forged in the creative process of mutual encounter and dialogue among members of different traditions and religious communities, it draws from their respective riches. A healing spirituality incorporates and cultivates all kinds of wisdom—Buddhist, Christian, Jewish, Muslim, Hindu, Sikh, the attitudes and worldviews of indigenous religions, and also values and principles of non-religious kinds of humanistic outlooks. Thus it enhances the sense of communion and empowerment among all individuals and communities across traditional boundaries, so that together, we can turn toward the tasks of reconciling with one another, overcoming our mutual as well as our inner alienation, and healing our wounded Earth.

More and more of us are seeking to cultivate such a healing spirituality in our individual lives. Empowered by our spiritual experience and nurtured in our own respective traditions, we can engage in the public forum with courage and conviction, addressing concrete issues that demand our attention. As we take up the tasks of "mending the world" (to borrow an expression from the Jewish tradition), we may see hopeful signs springing up among the debris of our wounded world.

A healing spirituality stems from a deepened awareness of our participation in the interconnected web of life we call Earth. Thus it shares the basic characteristics of an *ecological* spirituality. This refers to a way of life that cherishes and reveres Earth as the home and matrix of our shared life. It is manifested as a sensitivity to the sounds of Earth, a capacity to listen to and feel its pain as one's own, and a readiness to respond in ways that lead to healing. An ecological spirituality continues to take shape out of a shared vision of the many who—though perhaps in different ways and contexts—share the pain of Earth's manifold woundedness, and feel the urgent need to forge new directions in our modes of awareness and ways of living together on this planet.

This book has described key features of spiritual practice in the Zen tradition. This is a contemplative way of life centered on being still, listening to the breath, and calming the mind. In this state of stillness, we are able to open our eyes of wisdom, and see *things as they really are,* that is, without the obstructions of delusive attachments or false expectations. This ability to see things clearly opens us to an experience of intimate connectedness and communion with all living beings. Thus our heart and mind open out to embrace all beings as our kin. This connectedness is felt not just with human beings, but with all beings in our Earth community, past, present, and yet to come.

Grounded in this intimate sense of communion with all beings, we can experience their pain and suffering—as well as their joys— as our own. We are inspired and empowered to direct our life toward alleviating their pain and suffering, bringing about their well-being, and enhancing all that leads to joy and celebration.

As I have sought to describe throughout this book, the heart of Zen is the experience of awakening to the reality of our interconnectedness with the whole universe. This vision of interconnectedness is opened to us as we listen to the breath and surrender ourselves to its transformative power. Listening to the breath, the awakened person is able to hear the sounds of a wounded Earth, in their concrete manifestations in our fellow breathing beings. Thus we are empowered by the same breath to become an agent of healing. Responding to woundedness in whatever ways we can, we carry out our concrete tasks, based on our gifts, talents, and particular station in life.

Zen practice and spirituality as described in this book shares many features with other Buddhist contemplative traditions, including Insight meditation, or *vipassana;* the visualizations and other spiritual practices of the Tibetan tradition; and also the devotional practices of the Pure Land tradition. Several more volumes would be needed to spell this all out.

I have also sought to demonstrate that Zen spirituality resonates deeply with key features found in the Christian tradition: specifically, the contemplative way of life that confirms and deepens us in the central Christian commandment of love of God and love of neighbor, through devoted and selfless service—the theme of "contemplation in action."

Those seeking to cultivate a healing spirituality in their own lives will hopefully find guideposts in what is offered here. Those who are already engaged in some other form of spiritual practice—whether within or outside any of the traditional religious communities—may hopefully find elements that resonate with, corroborate, and confirm what they already know, cherish and uphold, in the healing breath of Zen.

NOTES

PREFACE

1. See the chapter entitled "The Zen Experience" in my *Experiencing Buddhism: Ways of Wisdom and Compassion* (Maryknoll, N.Y.: Orbis Books, 2005), pp. 108–128. For a panoramic and detailed historical account of Zen, I recommend the newly reissued book by Heinrich Dumoulin, *Zen Buddhism: A History*, 2 vols. (Bloomington, Indiana: World Wisdom, 2005), with critical and evaluative comments for each volume by John McRae and Victor Sogen Hori, two leading scholars of Zen today.

2. See Thomas Berry, *The Dream of the Earth* (San Francisco: Sierra Club Books, 1988), and also Anne Lonergan and Caroline Richards, eds., *Thomas Berry and the New Cosmology* (Mystic, Conn.: Twenty-Third Publications, 1987).

3. "Right view" is the first of the Noble Eightfold Path presented by the Buddha as a prescription for the healing of the ailing human condition. Our contention here is that the establishment of this "right view" would lead to the unfolding of the other steps called for in this healing process.

4. I also address these questions in *Living Zen, Loving God* (Boston: Wisdom Publications, 2004).

5. See Raimundo Panikkar, *The Intra-Religious Dialogue* (New York: Paulist Press, 1978). For theoretical implications of such a venture, see the very suggestive essay by Roger Corless, "The Mutual Fulfillment of Buddhism

and Christianity in Co-inherent Superconsciousness," in Paul Ingram and Frederick Streng, eds., *Buddhist Christian Dialogue: Mutual Renewal and Transformation* (Honolulu: University of Hawaii Press, 1986), pp. 115–136.

6. See Tosh Arai and Wesley Ariarajah, eds., *Spirituality in Interfaith Dialogue* (Maryknoll, N.Y.: Orbis Books, 1989), for a collection of essays based on actual experiences of intrareligious dialogue by persons from differing cultures. See also writings of Sr. Elaine MacInnes, Canadian-born Catholic nun and Zen Master, notably *Zen Contemplation: A Bridge of Living Water* (Ottawa: Novalis, 2001), as well as those of Robert Jinsen Kennedy, Jesuit Priest and Zen Master, notably *Zen Gifts to Christians* (New York: Crossroad, 2001). See also Harold Kasimov, Linda Kepplinger Keenan, and John Keenan, eds., *Beside Still Waters: Jews, Christians, and the Way of the Buddha* (Boston: Wisdom Publications, 2003), an award-winning collection featuring personal accounts of spirituality as cultivated in interreligious contexts.

CHAPTER 1. DIAGNOSING OUR WOUNDEDNESS

1. The twelve-step program of Alcoholics Anonymous, found so effective worldwide and now also adapted to deal with many other kinds of human situations in need of remedy, begins with the recognition and admission of the problem. For an adapted use of the twelve-step program for ecological action, see Albert LaChance, *Greenspirit—Twelve Steps in Ecological Spirituality* (Rockport, Mass.: Element, 1991).

2. The meeting of the Latin American Conference of Catholic Bishops held in Medellin, Colombia, in 1968, known as the Medellin Conference, following the spirit of Vatican II, which had just finished three years earlier, endorsed the involvement of the Roman Catholic Church in social issues in this continent and adopted the notion of "institutionalized violence" as "a voice crying out to the heavens for justice." For analyses of the structural nature of world poverty and hunger, see Susan George, *How the Other Half Dies—The Real Reasons for World Hunger* (Harmondsworth, U.K.: Penguin Books, 1986), and the same author's *A Fate Worse than Debt* (London: Penguin Books, 1988). Statistical data need updating, and a few items could stand revision in formulation, but George's presentation of the social, political, cultural, and economic structures of our global society highlights the stark imbalance of power, the unjust distribution of the goods of the earth as well as the deprivation of opportunities for decent human living among different sectors of the world's population, providing the reader with an integrated portrayal of the structures of violence that continue to wreak havoc in our world.

3. See David Loy, "Nonduality of Good and Evil: Buddhist Reflections on the New Holy War," in *The Great Awakening: A Buddhist Social Theory* (Boston: Wisdom Publications, 2004), pp. 103–119, and also his "Terror in the God-shaped Hole: A Buddhist Perspective on Modernity's Identity Crisis," in *Journal of Transpersonal Psychology* 36, no. 2 (2004), pp. 17–39.

4. This notion of humanity as the consciousness of Earth also derives from Thomas Berry. See his "Twelve Principles for Understanding the Universe and the Role of the Human in the Universe Process," in Lonergan and Richards, eds., *Thomas Berry and the New Cosmology*, pp. 107–108. Number 6 reads: "The human is that being in whom the universe activates, reflects upon, and celebrates itself in conscious awareness."

5. See the WorldWatch Institute, *State of the World 2005* (New York: Norton & Co.), which describes how "poverty, disease, environmental degradation, and competition over natural resources feed into global insecurity," and see the acute problem of global terrorism as symptomatic of more deeply rooted and far more broadly intertwined sets of problems than can be settled by applying military means. For assessments of the health, or rather the ailing condition, of our global society, see Edward O. Wilson, *The Future of Life* (New York: Alfred A. Knopf, 2002), Joseph Stiglitz, *Globalization and its Discontents* (New York: W. Norton & Co., 2002), Paul Ehrlich and Anne Ehrlich, *One With Nineveh: Politics, Consumption, and the Human Future* (Washington: Island Press, 2004).

6. The notion of "the Other" is a theme in recent thought highlighted especially in feminist and deconstructionist writings. See, for example, Simone de Beauvoir's classic *The Second Sex* (New York: Vintage Books, 1974), which develops the Sartrean thesis of "man as Self, woman as Other." See also Rebecca Tong, *Feminist Thought: A Comprehensive Introduction* (Boulder and San Francisco: Westview Press, 1989), especially Chapter 7, "Existentialist Feminism," pp. 195–216. I thank Prof. Millicent Feske, a former colleague at Perkins School of Theology, who now teaches at St. Joseph's University in Philadelphia, for her helpful comments in this regard.

7. For an account of the development of ideas on nature, see Max Oelschlaeger, *The Idea of the Wilderness—From Prehistory to the Age of Ecology* (New Haven and London: Yale University Press, 1991), especially Chapter 9, pp. 281–319. (I thank Emeritus Prof. Roy Hamric of the University of Texas at Arlington for introducing me to this book and its author.)

8. The lives of the founders of the different religious traditions of the world point to their familiarity with such a dimension from direct experience, which they have expressed in their own respective ways, based on differing

cultural contexts and conceptual presuppositions. Persons called "mystics," across various religious traditions, likewise attest to and live in this dimension that goes beyond the boundaries of our "ego-centered consciousness."

9. Martin Heidegger, *Introduction to Metaphysics* (New York: Anchor Books, 1959). His major work *Sein und Zeit (Being and Time)* is an exposition of this fundamental insight.

10. Martin Buber, *I and Thou* (New York: Scribner's, 1958).

11. Peter Berger, *The Sacred Canopy: Elements of a Sociological Theory of Religion* (Garden City, New York: Doubleday, 1967).

12. See Mark Juergensmeyer, *Terror in the Mind of God: The Global Rise of Religious Violence* (Berkeley: University of California Press, 2000); Charles Kimball, *When Religion Becomes Evil* (San Francisco: HarperSanFrancisco, 2002); Karen Armstrong, *Holy War: The Crusades and Their Impact on Today's World* (New York: Anchor Books, 2001); and Jessica Stern, *Terror in the Name of God: Why Religious Militants Kill* (New York: HarperCollins, 2003).

13. See for example Diana Eck, *A New Religious America* (San Francisco: HarperSanFrancisco, 2001) for a convincing and thought-provoking description of this situation of "world religions in our backyard."

14. See my *Experiencing Buddhism: Ways of Wisdom and Compassion* (New York: Orbis, 2005), pp. 37–40, for a treatment of these Four Ennobling Truths as a path to healing.

15. The work of Roman Catholic theologians Henri de Lubac, Karl Rahner, Edward Schillebeeckx, and others had developed this point since the time before the Second Vatican Council (1962–65). The movement known as Creation Spirituality led by Matthew Fox and colleagues takes up this insight and develops its implications in connection with contemporary issues, and also calls our attention to the works of Christian mystical writers echoing a similar theme.

CHAPTER 2. TASTING AND SEEING

1. For an account of the problematic regarding the status of Zen Ancestor Bodhidharma, see Heinrich Dumoulin, *Zen Buddhism: A History,* Vol. 1 (Bloomington, Ind.: World Wisdom, 2005), pp. 85–94. Recent studies have come out correcting and "demythologizing" some elements in Ch'an/Zen accounts of its own history, especially regarding the figure of Bodhidharma, and regarding the canonical lists of genealogical succession before the sixth Zen ancestor, Hui-neng. See Whalen Lai and Lewis Lancaster, eds., *Early Ch'an in China and Tibet* (Berkeley: Berkeley Buddhist Studies Series, 1983), and John McRae, *Seeing Through Zen: Encounter, Transformation, and Genealogy in Chinese Chan Buddhism* (Berkeley and Los Angeles: University of California Press, 2003)

2. For English translations with commentaries by twentieth-century Zen masters, see Zenkei Shibayama, *Zen Comments on the Mumonkan* (New York: New American Library, 1974), Koun Yamada, *Gateless Gate* (Boston: Wisdom Publications, 2004), and Robert Aitken, *The Gateless Barrier: Wu-men Kuan (Mu Mon Kan)* (San Francisco: North Point Press, 1991). For quotations used in this book, I have consulted these translations, freely adapting with my own as need arises to emphasize certain nuances.

3. Yamada, *Gateless Gate,* p. 39.

4. See Thomas Cleary, tr., *Transmission of Light (Denkoroku)* (San Francisco: North Point Press, 1990).

5. Yamada, *Gateless Gate,* p. 13.

6. Yamada, *Gateless Gate,* p. 147.

7. See Victor Sogen Hori, *Zen Sand: The Book of Capping Phrases for Koan Practice* (Honolulu: University of Hawaii Press, 2003).

8. See Philip Kapleau, *The Three Pillars of Zen* (Boston: Beacon Press, 1965), pp. 204–208. We will come back to this account of the Zen enlightenment experience later on in this book. See Chapter 6 of this book, titled "This Is My Body."

9. *Ibid.,* p. 238.

10. *Ibid.,* p. 244.

11. *Ibid.,* p. 250. Kapleau's book, edited and translated with the help of Yamada Koun, is based on the actual practice of the Zen Community of the Sanbo Kyodan, based in Kamakura, Japan. These testimonies derive from practitioners in this lineage. Another helpful work for beginners describing Zen practice based on this lineage is Robert Aitken, *Taking the Path of Zen* (San Francisco: North Point Press, 1982).

12. With the total emptying of the ego, the fullness of joy of being "in Christ" is an experience attested to by Christians. These testimonies, along with many others coming from direct experiences of this sort, with their differences in linguistic and conceptual content, challenge a thesis presented by Stephen Katz in his renowned essay "Language, Epistemology, and Mysticism," in Stephen Katz, ed., *Mysticism and Philosophical Analysis* (New York: Oxford University Press, 1978), pp. 22–74, wherein he categorically states that "there are NO pure (i.e. unmediated) experiences" (p. 26). The nature of these experiences of individuals from widely differing cultural backgrounds that continue to be confirmed in the Zen tradition is an issue that continues to be a matter of ongoing discussion among scholars. For corroboration from another Buddhist (i.e., the Tibetan) tradition of meditation, see Anne C. Klein, "Mental Concentration and the Unconditioned: A Buddhist Case for Unmediated Experience," in Robert E. Buswell and Robert M. Gimello, eds., *Paths to Liberation: The Marga and*

Its Transformations in Buddhist Thought (Honolulu: The Kuroda Institute, 1992), pp. 269–308. See also Hori, *Zen Sand,* especially his introductory chapter, on the nature of discourse about Zen experience.

13. Of the numerous works now available in English on this intriguing term "emptiness," I have found the work by Frederick J. Streng, *Emptiness: A Study in Religious Meaning* (Nashville: Abingdon Press, 1967), most helpful for conveying its significance to a Western audience. See also Keiji Nishitani, *Religion and Nothingness,* tr. Jan van Bragt (Berkeley and Los Angeles: University of California Press, 1982) for a very lucid philosophical treatment that may spark experiential insights. Jay L. Garfield, *The Fundamental Wisdom of the Middle Way: Nagarjuna's Mulamadhyamakakarika* (New York: Oxford University Press, 1995) is also recommended as an excellent rendition of second century Buddhist philosopher Nagarjuna's keynote treatise on Emptiness. For accounts of the issues on the ongoing debate on *shunyata,* see John B. Cobb and Christopher Ives, eds., *The Emptying God* (Maryknoll, N.Y.: Orbis Books, 1990); Roger Corless and Paul Knitter, eds., *Buddhist Emptiness and Christian Trinity* (New York: Paulist Press, 1990); Donald Mitchell, *Spirituality and Emptiness* (New York: Paulist Press, 1991), and James Fredericks, *Buddhists and Christians: Through Comparative Theology to Solidarity* (Maryknoll, N.Y.: Orbis Books, 2004.)

14. Yamada, *Gateless Gate,* p. 147.

15. Yasutani Hakuun Roshi (1885–1972) also had a significant role in the transplanting of the Zen tradition in the United States. See Rick Fields, *How the Swans Came to the Lake: A Narrative History of Buddhism in America,* revised and updated (Boulder: Shambhala, 1986), esp. pp. 231–272.

16. Aitken, *Gateless Barrier,* No. 41. Yamada, *Gateless Gate,* p. 208.

17. See the same preface to any volume of the series edited by Ewert Cousins, *World Spirituality: An Encyclopaedic History of the Religious Quest* (New York: Crossroad, 1988 and ff.).

18. Kapleau, *Three Pillars of Zen,* pp. 46–49. Rather than "aims" or "goals," words which still imply a separation of process and result, or "means and ends," I prefer to call these "the fruits of Zen practice."

19. Also see my *Living Zen, Loving God,* pp. 1–9.

20. My translation, from Dogen's essay entitled "Genjo-koan," which can be translated as "Actualizing Enlightenment," a chapter in his landmark *Shobogenzo* (The Eye Treasury of the True Dharma).

CHAPTER 3. LISTENING TO THE BREATH

1. Anthony Mottola, tr., *The Spiritual Exercises of St. Ignatius* (New York: Image Books, 1964), p. 61.

2. *Philokalia,* literally, "Love of the Beautiful and Good." This is a collection of spiritual writings dating from the 4th to the 15th century, dealing with what is known as Hesychasm and the Jesus Prayer. See Kadloubovsky and G. H. Palmer, tr., *Philokalia on Prayer of the Heart* (London: Faber & Faber, 1951), cited in William Johnston, *Christian Zen* (New York: Harper & Row, 1971), p. 80.

3. Mottola, *Spiritual Exercises,* p. 108.

4. See the *Collected Works of St. John of the Cross,* tr. Kieran Kavanaough, OCD, and Otilo Rodriguez, OCD (Washington, D.C.: Institute of Carmelite Studies, 1991), pp. 622–623 for another translation.

5. Fr. Lassalle's pioneering work introducing Christians to Zen practice is noted worldwide. See his *Zen Meditation for Christians* (New York: Open Court, 1974). See also his *Living in the New Consciousness* (Boston: Shambhala, 1988).

6. Aitken, *Gateless Barrier,* No. 37.

CHAPTER 4. AWAKENING TO TRUE SELF

1. See Jon Kabat-Zinn, *Full Catastrophe Living* (New York: Dell Publishing Co., 1990), and also his more recent *Coming to Our Senses: Healing Ourselves and the World Through Mindfulness.* (New York: Hyperion, 2005)

2. In Chinese, this response is pronounced "Wu," but this koan has come to be known in the West taking the Japanese pronunciation of Chao-chou (Joshu)'s retort (Mu), in itself an opaque sound which has served well in cutting through the discursive intellect and spurring Zen practice. Yamada, *Gateless Gate,* No. 1.

3. For transcriptions of Zen talks or *teisho* on the koan *mu* and how one applies it in practice, see Yasutani Hakuun's commentary excerpted in Kapleau, *Three Pillars,* pp. 63–82; Yamada, *Gateless Gate,* pp. 13–18; Aitken, *The Gateless Barrier,* pp. 7–18.

4. Aitken, *The Gateless Barrier,* pp. 7–9.

5. See Kapleau, ed., *Three Pillars,* pp. 54–57.

6. See the series of negations in the *Heart Sutra,* a short text chanted as part of Zen practice in different languages in Zen halls all over the world. These negations have been systematized in Buddhist logic with the second century philosopher Nagarjuna's so-called dialectic of the Four Negations. Jay Garfield's *Fundamental Wisdom of the Middle Way* (cited above) presents Nagarjuna's arguments in a systematic way, with helpful commentaries.

7. See Chapter 2, n. 13, above.

8. Martin Heidegger, *Introduction to Metaphysics*, p. 86ff.
9. T. S. Eliot, *Collected Poems, 1909–1962* (London: Faber and Faber, Ltd., 1963), p. 222.
10. Dogen Zenji, *Shobogenzo: The Eye and the Treasury of the True Law,* Vol. 1, tr. Kosen Nishiyama and John Stevens (Tokyo: Nakayama Shobo, 1975), p. 154.
11. Paul Tillich, "You Are Accepted," in *Shaking the Foundations* (New York: Charles Scribner's Sons, 1948), pp. 159–169. I thank Fr. Rafael Davila, M.M., of the Maryknoll Education Center in Houston, Texas, for calling my attention to and sending me a copy of this essay.

CHAPTER 5. EMBODYING THE WAY

1. Aitken, *Gateless Barrier,* No. 7.
2. There is a movement now among Zen Teachers in North America to reclaim the place of the women ancestors in Buddhist history. Some practice centers, including the San Francisco Zen Center, and others, now include a list of women among those honored as ancestors in the line of Zen transmission.
3. See Patrick Henry and Donald Swearer, *For the Sake of the World: The Spirit of Buddhist and Christian Monasticism* (Minneapolis, Minn.: Fortress Press, and Collegeville, Minn.: The Liturgical Press, 1989), for a comparative account of monasticism in Buddhist and Christian traditions.
4. There is a regular newsletter issued by this association, based at the Benedictine Osage Monastery of Peace at Sand Springs, Oklahoma, and the Trappist Abbey of Gethsemani, Kentucky.
5. The community at Zen Mountain Monastery in Mt. Tremper, New York, as well as San Francisco Zen Center and its affiliates at Green Gulch and Tassajara, California, can be seen as forging models in this regard. The community at St. Katharina-werk near Zurich, in Switzerland, headed by Sr. Pia Gyger, a Catholic religious who is also a Zen disciple of Yamada Koun Roshi and Robert Aitken Roshi, is another group experimenting with different forms of communal life with an orientation to tasks of reconciliation in the socioecological fields. For descriptions of contemporary forms of Buddhist monastic life in the Western hemisphere, see James Ishmael Ford, *A Brief History of Zen: Tracing the Tradition from Ancient India to Modern America* (Boston: Wisdom Publications, 2006).
6. For an account of this interplay of fullness/emptiness, see *Living Zen, Loving God,* pp. 11–25.
7. Aitken, *Gateless Barrier,* No. 41.
8. See Shunryu Suzuki, *Zen Mind, Beginner's Mind* (New York and Tokyo: Weatherhill, 1970), for an account of Zen spirituality as the cultivation of "beginner's mind."

9. See videotape released by Innergrowth Books, Box 520, Chiloquin, OR 97624, featuring Susan Jion Postal's Zen Journey. *(www.innergrowth.com)*

10. Chögyam Trungpa, *Cutting Through Spiritual Materialism* (Boulder and London: Shambhala, 1973).

11. Kavanaugh and Rodriguez, eds., *Collected Works of St. John of the Cross,* pp. 365–367.

12. The noted scandals related to sexual and financial improprieties of certain meditation teachers in the United States make us all too aware of the pitfalls in this regard on the part of both disciple and teacher. For a revealing account, see Michael Downing, *Shoes Outside the Door: Desire, Devotion, and Excess at San Francisco Zen Center* (Washington, D.C.: Counterpoint, 2001.)

13. Anchor Books edition, p. 3.

14. Morris Berman, *The Reenchantment of the World* (Ithaca, N.Y.: Cornell University Press, 1981, republished by Bantam Books, 1984).

15. An account of this incident is included in David Friend and the editors of *Life, The Meaning of Life—Reflections in Words and Pictures on Why We Are Here* (Boston: Little, Brown and Co., 1991), p. 187.

CHAPTER 6. THIS IS MY BODY

1. See Zenkei Shibayama's commentary in *A Flower Does Not Talk: Zen Essays,* tr. Sumiko Kudo (Rutland, Vt.: Charles Tuttle & Co., 1970), pp. 65–67.

2. See *Living Zen, Loving God,* Chapter 5, pp. 51–70, for a commentary on the Song of Zazen.

3. See the *Genjokoan* ("The Matter at Hand") chapter of Dogen's *Shobogenzo.* This is my own translation from the Japanese.

4. Maurice Merleau-Ponty's work, *Phenomenology of Perception* (New York: Humanities Press, 1962) is a noted landmark in this regard, and it was followed by other works from different philosophical and theological traditions, leading to a new awareness of bodiliness that overcomes the dualistic setting of Descartes and the "modern" thought that followed. For a collection of essays outlining major strands on thinking about the body, see Stuart F. Spieker, *The Philosophy of the Body—Rejections of Cartesian Dualism* (Chicago: Quadrangle Books, 1970).

5. See Yuasa Yasuo, *The Body: Toward an Eastern Mind-Body Theory,* ed. T. P. Kasulis (New York: State University of New York Press, 1987), and David Edward Shaner, *The BodyMind Experience in Japanese Buddhism—A Phenomenological Study of Kukai and Dogen* (New York: State University of New York Press, 1985).

6. Pp. 204–208, listed as "A Japanese Executive, K. Y., age 47."

7. The chapter on *"Sokushin-Soku Butsu"* ("This very mind, the Buddha") of Dogen's *Shobogenzo*. See Nishiyama and Stevens, Vol. 1, p. 17, for a variation.

8. See *Living Zen, Loving God,* Chapter 3, pp. 27–44.

9. See Shibayama, *Zen Comments on the Mumonkan,* p. 10.

10. Thomas Cleary, tr., *The Book of Serenity* (New York: Lindisfarne Press, 1990), Case 91, p. 390.

11. See Ken Wilber, ed., *The Holographic Paradigm and Other Paradoxes: Exploring the Leading Edges of Science* (Boston and London: Shambhala, 1982). Karl Pribram's work is published in his *Languages of the Brain* (1971), and developed in synthesis with David Bohm's work in G. Globus, et al., eds., *Consciousness and the Brain* (New York: Plenum, 1976), and R. Shaw and J. Bransford, eds., *Perceiving, Acting, and Knowing* (New York: John Wiley, 1977). David Bohm's work is presented in Ted Bastin, ed., *Quantum Theory and Beyond* (New York: Cambridge University Press, 1971), and in *Foundations of Physics,* Vols. 1(4), 3(2), and 5(1).

12. See Francis Cook, *Hua-Yen Buddhism: The Jewel Net of Indra* (University Park, Penn. and London: Pennsylvania State University Press, 1981).

CHAPTER 7. COMING HOME

1. Thich Nhat Hanh, *The Miracle of Mindfulness* (Boston: Beacon Books, 1970), pp. 3–5.

2. The coincidence of the *already* and the *not yet* characterizes the dynamic of the reign of God in our lives. In such a context, a *realized eschatology* such as that manifested in the fourth Gospel is not an oxymoron but is precisely an incidence of this "coincidence of opposites." For a further development of this theme, see my essay on "The Resurrection of the Body and Life Everlasting: From a Futuristic to a Realized Christianity," in Paul Ingram and Sallie King, eds., *The Sound of Liberating Truth: Essays in Honor of Frederick J. Streng* (Surrey, England: Curzon Press, 1999), pp. 223–243.

3. In contrast to his detailed instructions on the vow of obedience and also on poverty, he brushes off this aspect with a few curt remarks. See his *Rules for the Society of Jesus.*

4. Frank Bottomley, *Attitudes to the Body in Western Christendom* (London: Lepus Books, 1979), provides a good historical account of the development of thought on the body in Christianity.

5. See Spieker, ed., *The Philosophy of the Body—Rejections of Cartesian Dualism.*

6. See, for example, Charles Davis, *Body as Spirit* (London: 1976), for a theological perspective. Matthew Fox, *Sins of the Spirit, Blessings of the Flesh: Lessons for Transforming Evil in Soul and Society* (New York: Three Rivers

Press, 1999) is an insightful treatment inviting us to a recovery of our bodiliness as the locus of the Holy.

7. See F. X. Durwell, *The Resurrection* (London: Sheed and Ward, 1960), for a landmark study in this regard, based on reflection on scriptural sources.

8. See David Shaner, *The BodyMind Experience in Japanese Buddhism*, especially the section on Dogen, pp. 129–185.

9. Shibayama, *A Flower Does Not Talk*, pp. 65–67.

10. See Erich Neumann, *Depth Psychology and a New Ethic* (New York: G.P. Putnam's Sons, 1969), especially Appendix 1, "Reflections on the Shadow," pp. 137–147.

11. *Ibid.,* pp. 34–35.

12. *Ibid.,* pp. 50–58.

13. See Ernst Becker, *The Denial of Death* (San Francisco: Harper & Row, 1973).

14. These reflections on the shadow deserve much more detailed treatment than we can present in summary form in this chapter, in terms of the tremendous significance its understanding can bring regarding our human patterns of behavior. The contribution of Jungian psychology in elucidating this area is of course significant, and the insights of Eastern religious traditions, notably Tibetan Tantric Buddhism, can be further explored in this connection. For example, there are meditative exercises of visualization focusing on evil or demonic figures that are recommended in this tradition, and such exercises are powerful ways of reconciling the practitioner with one's shadow. I am grateful to Dr. Adelheid Herrmann-Pfandt, of the University of Marburg, Germany, for calling my attention to this theme, which she dealt with in an unpublished paper entitled "The Logic of Love: The Peace Policy of the Dalai Lama, Its Origin and Its Consequences." See also Herbert Guenther, *The Tantric View of Life* (Berkeley and London: Shambhala, 1972).

See also David Loy, *Lack and Transcendence: The Problem of Death and Life in Psychotherapy, Existentialism, and Buddhism* (Atlantic Highlands, N.J.: Humanities Press, 1996) and his *A Buddhist History of the West—Studies in Lack* (Albany: State University of New York Press, 2002). See also Robert A. Johnson, *Owning Your Own Shadow: Understanding the Dark Side of the Psyche* (San Francisco: HarperSanFrancisco, 1991).

15. Attributed to Irenaeus of Lyons (c. 130–c. 200).

16. Feminist and womanist writers, especially in the last two decades, have thrown light on the patriarchal structures in our human attitudes and institutions. See Rosemarie Tong, *Feminist Thought: A Comprehensive Introduction* (Boulder and San Francisco: Westview Press, 1989). Mary Daly, *Beyond God the Father—Toward a Philosophy of Women's Liberation* (Boston:

Beacon Press, 1973), has pointed out how Christian male-centered imagery of the divine is inseparably rooted in such structures.

17. See *Living Zen, Loving God,* Chapter 9, "Kuan Yin with a Thousand Hands," pp. 93–101.

18. Walter M. Abbott, S.J., *The Documents of Vatican II* (New York: Guild Press, 1966), p. 92.

19. See Sallie McFague, *Models of God—Theology for an Ecological, Nuclear Age* (Philadelphia: Fortress Press, 1987), especially pp. 97–123, and Leonardo Boff, *The Maternal Face of God: The Feminine and Its Religious Expressions* (San Francisco: Harper & Row, 1987), among others, for explorations on this theme. We can look to Zen for further contributions in this area, as practitioners also conversant with Christian imagery give expression to the manifold dimensions of their Zen experience in terms consonant with the biblical tradition.

20. The noted lecture of Lynn White, Jr., entitled "The Historic Roots of Our Ecologic Crisis," *Science* 155 (1967), pp. 1203–1207, referred to "orthodox Christian arrogance toward nature," and pointed to the Genesis story as a basis for the exploitative attitude humans have taken toward the natural world. White's essay has sparked a lively controversy also among Christian circles. See also H. Paul Santmire, *The Travail of Nature—The Ambiguous Ecological Promise of Christian Theology* (Philadelphia: Fortress Press, 1985) for a historical investigation of Christian views toward the natural world. See also William Leiss, *The Domination of Nature* (New York: George Braziller, 1972).

21. The need to go beyond "stewardship," which still rings of an anthropocentric attitude, is beginning to be emphasized among some circles, although "mainline" Christians would still hold on to this as at least a way to overcome the "subjugation and domination" attitude derived from the Genesis story. See Wesley Granberg-Michaelson, *Ecology and Life: Accepting Our Environmental Responsibility* (Waco, Tex.: Word Books, 1988); Anne Rowthorn, *Caring for Creation* (Wilton, Conn: Morehouse Publishing, 1989); Art and Jocele Meyer, *Earthkeepers—Environmental Perspectives on Hunger, Poverty and Injustice* (Scottdale, Penn: Herald Press, 1991), among others. See also Dieter Hessell and Rosemary Radford Ruether, eds., *Christianity and Ecology: Seeking the Well-being of Earth and Humans* (Cambridge: Harvard University Center for the Study of World Religions, 2000).

22. See Thomas Berry, *Befriending the Earth—A Theology of Reconciliation Between Humans and the Earth,* with Thomas Clarke, S.J. (Mystic, Conn.: Twenty-Third Publications, 1991).

23. Dialogue and cooperation among members of different religious traditions on this shared task is now being seen as of crucial importance. See Sean

McDonagh, *To Care for the Earth* (Santa Fe: Bear & Co., 1990); Eugene C. Hargrove, *Religion and the Environmental Crisis* (Athens, Ga., and London: The University of Georgia Press, 1986). See especially Jay McDaniel, *With Roots and Wings: Christianity in an Age of Ecology and Dialogue* (New York: Orbis Books, 1995). See also the series on world religions and ecology issued by Harvard University's Center for the Study of World Religions, published by Cambridge University Press.

24. This perspective is presented by Christian theologians inspired by the Process thought of Alfred North Whitehead, Charles Hartshorne, and others. See also Jay McDaniel's essay entitled "Revisioning God and the Self," in Charles Birch, William Eakin, and Jay McDaniel, eds., *Liberating Life: Contemporary Approaches to Ecological Theology* (Maryknoll, N.Y.: Orbis Books, 1990), pp. 228–258.

25. Gary Snyder, *The Practice of the Wild* (San Francisco: North Point Press, 1990), is a recent collection that is noteworthy in this regard. Gary Snyder's influence on American thinking on nature is evaluated by Max Oelschlaeger in *The Idea of Wilderness* (New Haven, Conn.: Yale University Press, 1991), Chapter 8, pp. 243–280.

26. For a thought-provoking essay, see Frederick Turner, "Cultivating the American Garden," in *Rebirth of Value: Meditations on Beauty, Ecology, Religion, and Education* (New York: State University of New York Press, 1991), pp. 51–63.

27. See Ruben L.F. Habito, *Experiencing Buddhism: Ways of Wisdom and Compassion.* (New York: Orbis Books, 2005), p. 19.

EPILOGUE

1. I develop this further in my essay entitled "The Inner Pursuit of Happiness," in Stephanie Kaza, ed., *Hooked!—Buddhist Writings on Greed, Desire, and the Urge to Consume* (Boston: Shambhala, 2005), pp. 34–48.

2. The Worldwatch Institute's *State of the World, 2005* edition, is subtitled *Redefining Global Insecurity,* emphasizing the interrelatedness of the major challenges facing our world today: "the challenge of security, including the risks associated with weapons of mass destruction and terrorism; the challenge of poverty and underdevelopment; and the challenge of environmental sustainability" (p. xvii).

Index

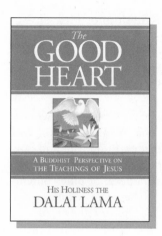

The Good Heart
A Buddhist Perspective on the Teachings of Jesus
His Holiness the Dalai Lama
224 pages
Cloth: ISBN 0-86171-114-9, $24.00
Paper: ISBN 0-86171-138-6, $15.95

The Dalai Lama provides an extraordinary Buddhist perspective on the teachings of Jesus, commenting on well-known passages from the four Christian Gospels including the Sermon on the Mount, the parable of the mustard seed, the Resurrection, and others.

"Arguably the best book on interreligious dialogue published to date. One does not say such things lightly, but in a very real sense this is a holy book."—Huston Smith, author of *The Illustrated World's Religions*

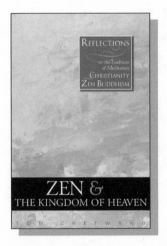

Zen and the Kingdom of Heaven
Reflections on the Tradition of Meditation in Christianity and Zen Buddhism
Tom Chetwynd
224 pages, ISBN 0-86171-187-4, $16.95

This provocative and very human work is the story of one man's skeptical first encounters with Zen Buddhism and how it led him to the rich—but largely forgotten—Christian tradition of pure contemplative prayer. Chetwynd explores the surprisingly Zen-like teachings of the Desert Fathers and other Christian meditation masters whose practice stems from the very first Christian communities—and perhaps Jesus Christ himself.

"An excellent publication that presents the personal and direct interface of Buddhism and Christianity. Part One, 'Zen Experience,' has all the dynamics and inspiration of genuine experience and is well worth the price of the book. Part Two, 'Christian Meditation in the Light of Zen,' traces the story of Christian meditation and its line of teachers right up to the present....The quotations given are outstanding...Part Three goes into practical details about Christians doing Zen, giving concrete suggestions for practice....We simply need more books like this one."—*Bulletin of Monastic Interreligious Dialogue*

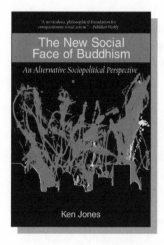

The New Social Face of Buddhism
An Alternative Sociopolitical Perspective
Ken Jones | Foreword by Kenneth Kraft
320 pages, ISBN 0-86171-365-6, $16.95

Jones presents an astute, well-informed, and balanced analysis of the philosophy, history, and future of socially relevant Buddhism. *The New Social Face of Buddhism* is vital reading for activists, scholars, and everyone seeking to transform their spiritual practice into a force for social, political, and global change. A groundbreaking book, Jones' work is a wellspring of inspiration that should not be missed.

"A meticulous, philosophical foundation for compassionate social action."—*Publishers Weekly*

Living Zen, Loving God
Ruben L.F. Habito
Foreword by John Keenan
160 pages, ISBN 0-86171-383-4, $14.95

"Christians who practice meditation and especially Zen-curious Christians should not miss this book. Habito's reading of the Enlightened Samaritan story alone is worth the price of admission."—The Rev. Deacon Kenneth Arnold, author of *Nightfishing in Galilee*

"No one is more qualified than Ruben Habito to write such a book."—David R. Loy, author of *The Great Awakening: A Buddhist Social Theory*

"This is theology as it should be."—Kim Boykin, author of *Zen for Christians*

About Wisdom Publications

Wisdom Publications, a nonprofit publisher, is dedicated to making available authentic works relating to Buddhism for the benefit of all. We publish books by ancient and modern masters in all traditions of Buddhism, translations of important texts, and original scholarship. Additionally, we offer books that explore East-West themes unfolding as traditional Buddhism encounters our modern culture in all its aspects. Our titles are published with the appreciation of Buddhism as a living philosophy, and with the special commitment to preserve and transmit important works from Buddhism's many traditions.

To learn more about Wisdom, or to browse books online, visit our website at www.wisdompubs.org.

You may request a copy of our catalog online or by writing to this address:

Wisdom Publications
199 Elm Street
Somerville, Massachusetts 02144 USA
Telephone: 617-776-7416
Fax: 617-776-7841
Email: info@wisdompubs.org
www.wisdompubs.org

THE WISDOM TRUST

As a nonprofit publisher, Wisdom is dedicated to the publication of Dharma books for the benefit of all sentient beings and dependent upon the kindness and generosity of sponsors in order to do so. If you would like to make a donation to Wisdom, you may do so through our website or our Somerville office. If you would like to help sponsor the publication of a book, please write or email us at the address above.

Thank you.

Wisdom is a nonprofit, charitable 501(c)(3) organization affiliated with the Foundation for the Preservation of the Mahayana Tradition (FPMT).